Mickey Mantle
The Yankee Years

The Classic Photography of Ozzie Sweet

Text by Larry Canale • Foreword by Whitey Ford

Tuff Stuff Books

Published by Tuff Stuff Publications, 1934 E. Parham Road, Richmond, Virginia 23228.
Tuff Stuff Books and Tuff Stuff Publications are divisions of Landmark Specialty Publications Inc.

To order additional copies of this book, or to request a free catalog, please contact
Tuff Stuff Books, P.O. Box 1050, Dubuque, Iowa 52004, or call (800) 334-7165.

Library of Congress Cataloging-in-Publication Data
Canale, Larry.
Mickey Mantle: the Yankee years: the classic photography of Ozzie Sweet/
text by Larry Canale: foreword by Whitey Ford: design by Tim Roberts.

ISBN: 0-930625-21-8

1. Sports—Baseball—Pictorial works.
I. Sweet, Ozzie. I. Title

Library of Congress Catalog Number: 98-87758

Editorial Director: Larry Canale
Copy Editor: John Harrington
Statistics/Research: Matt Smith

Design Director/Graphic Design: Tim Roberts
Graphic Design: Fred Wollenberg

Typeface: Baskerville (primary) and Univers (secondary)
Color separations: Graphic Art Services, Richmond, Virginia
Printed in the United States of America.

Cover photograph: Ozzie Sweet
Cover design: Tim Roberts

Pictured on p. 1: Ozzie Sweet with his view camera in a mid-1950s photograph.
Pictured on p. 6: Ozzie Sweet and a wall of Sport *covers he photographed.*

Dedications

To my wife Diane, my daughters Pamela and Linnea, and my son Blair. I'm truly thankful for their love and support back through the years.

—Ozzie Sweet

To my wife Lauren and to my parents, Larry Sr. and Millie, for their encouragement and inspiration.

—Larry Canale

Acknowledgements

The author first must extend heartfelt appreciation and respect to Ozzie Sweet for his cooperation, advice, and especially his wonderful photography. Ozz, you're a joy to work with.

I also owe thanks to everyone at Tuff Stuff Publications, especially the editors— Keith Gentili, Doug Scoville, John Harrington, Tom DeZego, Jerry Shaver, Andi Lucas, and Michael Litos—for keeping the ball rolling during this book's production. Special thanks to Harrington for copy editing these pages, DeZego for his typography assistance, and production manager Art Dixon for his help in mapping out this book. Thanks also to Jim Warren and his price guide crew (Melanie Haynie, Jeremy Zucker, Bill Beaman, and Dorothy Holt) and to TSP's talented designers (especially Gordon Schmidt, Abe Longmire, Randy Stepanek, and Samantha Tannich) for being automatic.

Thanks to TSP president Frank Finn and to Landmark Specialty Publications president Rick Spears for their roles in this project's development. Thanks to TSP's Matt Smith for his stats-compiling and all-around "utility" help. Thanks also to Cam Smith, a true-blue Yankee fan who provided key research material.

I also must offer kind thanks to Yankee historian Marty Appel, who added his expertise to this book's content. Thanks to writer David Seideman for the useful research library, and to Richard Bond of Leland's for uncovering the wonderful Mickey Mantle–signed Sweet photo on p. 215. Thanks to "Slick," Whitey Ford, for his contributions. And thanks to the Mantle family, especially David and Danny Mantle, for their support.

Special thanks to Fred Wollenberg for the care and finesse he put into this book's design—and the speed with which he completed it. Truly a job well-done. The fine folks at Graphic Art Services—especially Warren "Doc" Van Hook and John Myers—also deserve kudos for their vital work in restoring the color in these aging transparencies while preserving the integrity of Ozzie's work.

Finally, I offer very special thanks and admiration to Tim Roberts for the quality he's given this book—and for the calm he exhibited during a tight deadline. His thoughtful design direction has provided Ozzie's remarkable images with the classy setting they deserve.

—L.C.

Contents

Thanks for the Memories

Thirty years I waited. Thirty long years.

Earlier this year, in January 1998, photographer Ozzie Sweet finally delivered a set of black-and-white prints he promised to me—way back in 1956. The pictures were from a deep-sea fishing trip Ozzie set up after spring training that year. I have great memories of that trip, because my friends Mickey Mantle, Billy Martin, and Bob Grim were all there, too. We each caught something, although I

recall my fish being the biggest. (Later in this book, Ozzie remembers Billy reeling in the day's biggest catch. Don't believe him.)

Now, I remember a lot of things about that trip. The battles with the fish. The cool waves. The good stories. And my need to pick up a ladies' hat (it was from a dress shop, the only place open near the dock) to wear on the boat to protect me from the sun. What doesn't stand out so much is Ozzie Sweet—but only because he didn't bring his usual load of photography gear along. He just had a

small camera, and he snapped a roll or two of film while we fished and relaxed.

See, we were all used to the big, bulky view camera Ozzie used to photograph us ballplayers. Every year, spring training was overrun with photographers, but Ozzie always stood out. We could spot him a mile away because of his old-fashioned camera and the cases full of equipment and props he'd set up.

Whitey Ford—as a player (left) and coach—is one of dozens of Yankees Ozzie Sweet immortalized on film.

Back in the 1950s and '60s, Ozzie was well-known for his pictures inside and on the cover of *Sport* magazine. It was a big deal for a player to get featured on *Sport*'s cover. Remember, there weren't many sports magazines at the time, and there was no ESPN telling you everything you wanted to know about your heroes. *Sport* was one of the few national publications devoted to the topic; it certainly was one of the most prestigious. And if you got chosen to be on a *Sport* cover, it almost always meant you'd be working with Ozzie.

Ozzie was always organized, so his photo sessions usually came off smoothly and quickly. He would arrange things ahead of time, and before you got there, he'd already have his props and equipment all set up. You could get in and out within 10 or 20 minutes. You could tell Ozzie always put a lot of thought into what he was doing, and that he always knew exactly what he wanted.

Mickey was baseball's brightest star in the 1950s and '60s, so he sat for more Ozzie Sweet pictures than any of us. Some guys didn't like sitting through any kind of photo shoot, never mind Ozzie's, but Mickey always did it without complaining. That's probably why so many of Ozzie's pictures of Mickey came out so well. The portraits of him in this book are as close as you could possibly get to Mickey. When you look through these pages, you'll see what I mean.

Any true baseball fan will enjoy seeing Mickey as he progressed through his career. You'll also enjoy Ozzie's pictures of so many other Yankees—Joe D., Tommy Henrich, Phil Rizzuto, and Casey Stengel; Yogi and Billy and me; and Ralph Terry, Joe Pepitone, and Bobby Murcer.

But for me, it's the fishing trip photos that bring back the fondest memories. They practically put me back out there in the Gulf of Mexico, joking around with my best friends, not a care in the world.

It was after we got back to the dock that I asked Ozzie to send me a set of pictures from the trip. Apparently, he forgot. For 30 years. But I won't hold a grudge—better late than never, right?

Thanks for the memories, Ozzie. They were well worth the wait.

Whitey Ford

Discovering Ozzie Sweet

For 11 years, I lived in picturesque southern New Hampshire—just a 15-minute drive from the home of legendary photographer Ozzie Sweet. Because I worked in the field of music journalism for most of those 11 years, however, my path never crossed his.

At Christmastime in 1993, just after I'd relocated to Richmond, Virginia, to edit the national sports collectibles magazine *Tuff Stuff,* I received a gift I've practically worn out. One of my editor friends, Dan Sullivan, presented me with an autographed copy of *Legends of the Field/The Classic Sports Photography of Ozzie Sweet* (Viking/Penguin).

What a book! It's filled with lively color images of the most important athletes of the 1950s and 1960s. The book accomplished exactly what writer Steve Wulf promised. It brought to life all of those unforgettable photographs Ozzie Sweet shot for *Sport* magazine in its formative years—photos that I (and millions of other young sports fans) studied, saved, and memorized. In *Legends of the Field,* Sweet's photography was reborn, and it more than stood the test of time. It survived like fine art should.

Mickey Mantle, of course, showed up in several photos among the hundreds that graced *Legends of the Field.* So in 1994, when I decided to feature Mantle on a *Tuff Stuff* cover, I figured I'd go with the best: a Sweet classic. I contacted Ozzie to ask about using his photography and quickly found out what an endearing gentleman he is—friendly, warm, and full of kind, sincere words. I also discovered he has a great memory, and that he especially enjoyed reminiscing about "The Mick." He photographed Mantle nearly every year of his career, from the Yankee legend's baby-faced early years to his 1968 swan song.

We ended up using my own favorite shot of Mantle on the cover of the September 1994 *Tuff Stuff.* It's a photo Sweet set up late in the 1966 baseball season, and it captures a mature, well-tanned Mantle in his Yankee cap and those bright pinstripes. Weeks later, I wasn't surprised to learn that the September 1994 *Tuff Stuff* became one of our best-selling issues ever.

A few months later, I visited New Hampshire and arranged to meet Sweet in person. The farmhouse in which he and his wife

Sweet checks in with Mantle in 1991. Each is holding a Sports Illustrated *containing a Sweet photo essay.*

Diane live is every bit as inviting as Ozzie and every bit as classic as his photography. Today, he remains active as a lensman, photographing vintage automobiles as well as domestic animals for use in ongoing calendar series. In the deliberate stagings he creates in and around his home, and in shooting classic cars, he takes great pains in pulling together even more elaborate setups that include people in costume and props that always fit (see p. 36 for examples).

But it's Ozzie's sports photography that keeps me coming back to his catalog. In fact, I've dipped into his portfolio four more times for *Tuff Stuff* covers—May 1995 (Ted Williams), November 1995 (Mantle), March 1998 (a Roberto

Clemente gem), and November 1998 (Mantle and Roger Maris).

In preparing the text for this book, I worked closely with Ozzie and got to know him and Diane (who frequently models in his classic car photos) even better. Gradually, the types of things I read in my research hit home.

Thomas P. Orr, photo editor of *Newsweek*, once wrote, "Ozzie never loses his sense of humor, no matter how trying the situation."

James Borcherding, senior editor of *Successful Farming*, wrote, "Ozzie likes people, they like him…. He's bright, cheerful, and has the sincere charm that warms the response of his photo subjects."

Ed Fitzgerald, former editor of *Sport*, wrote in the *Legends of the Field* Introduction: "Ozzie combined technical skill with creative virtuosity, but his true talent, the spark that fired his genius, was his buoyant personality. Like Will Rogers, Ozzie never met a man he didn't like, or a woman either, and he could charm the birds out of trees. Even if you were a reluctant subject who began the session grumbling that you had a million better things to do than pose for another batch of pictures by another pushy photographer, you ended up being Ozzie's friend."

It's important to note that Sweet's persona is not an act. How else could he get so much cooperation from so many different people (including some with fairly large egos) over a 55-year span?

One of his subjects, Leo Durocher, is notorious for his "Nice guys finish last" quote. Ozzie Sweet blows that theory all to hell.

Meeting Mickey Mantle

In July 1994, Mickey Mantle came to Richmond to appear at a *Tuff Stuff* collectibles show. "The Mick" was contracted to sign autographs for a three-hour period. In the process, he would create the thrill of a lifetime for more than

700 fans. It was an important week-end for me because Mantle also agreed to an interview. He invited me to The Jefferson Hotel the morning of his appearance and gave me an hour of his time. Some of the material from our discussion appears within these pages and helps put the pictures in context.

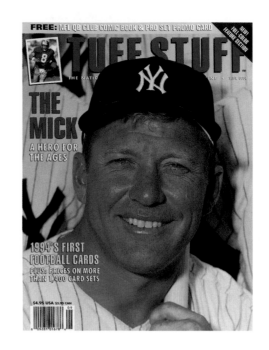

Mantle talked about a variety of topics, including his relationship with the paternal Casey Stengel, his commitment to switch-hitting, his regret that his lifetime batting average fell below .300 in his final season, and his take on the designated hitter as it relates to today's game. He also talked about how he enjoyed meeting his fans during his various autograph appearances: "I have guys come through and they get tears in their eyes, and they say, 'Mickey, I've waited 30 years to meet you! You can't believe it.' And they'll have their kids with them, and they'll say, 'Son, this is Mickey Mantle, the greatest play-er….' Hell, I get goosebumps sometimes just talking to these guys."

By the time of our interview, Mantle had answered every type of question that could possibly have been tossed at him. Yet he graciously and respectfully responded with serious and thoughtful answers to every question I asked. And I appreciated that.

Roughly a year later, Mantle passed away at just 63 years old.

At *Tuff Stuff*, we planned a tribute that would appear in our November 1995 issue. Our choice of photography: another portrait from Ozzie Sweet's catalog.

I called Sweet just after Mantle's passing, and he spoke at length of their unique relationship. He talked about how Mickey cooperated with him during each of their many photo sessions, and about how Mantle used to greet him at the start of spring training every year. He can still hear Mantle's voice, even 40 years later: *"Hey Ozz! What kind of stuff are we gonna do this year?"*

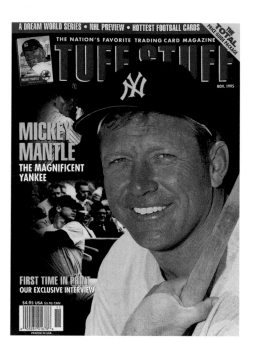

"It made me feel good to know that he recognized me, and that he looked forward to whatever I had in store for him," Sweet said.

The more Ozzie talked, the more emotional he got. He had to pause for a moment, perhaps reliving one of those long-ago photo sessions under the hot sun in Florida, the ace *Sport* magazine photographer positioning the nation's most popular athlete in front of a giant view camera.

Tuff Stuff helped sports collectors rediscover Ozzie Sweet's Mantle in two mid-1990s issues.

"He was a good guy," Sweet said. "He was too young...."

It wasn't long after that call that Ozzie and I began discussing the project you're holding. Sweet had enough Mantle material from 1952 through 1968 to give baseball fans a precise photographic record of Mickey as he matured during his career.

As a fan of Sweet's work and a Yankee loyalist myself, I *wanted* a book like this—one that provides a cohesive, chronological journey through Mickey's long playing career, an intimate look into the eyes of one of our greatest sports heroes.

At the same time, these pages reflect the fact that Ozzie Sweet, in his own way, has immortalized the Mickey Mantle we remember most fondly: the muscular, forever-young ballplayer wearing No. 7 and hitting those titanic home runs.

Introduction

The Making of a Photographer

How does life prepare a man to become the premier sports photographer of his generation? What sets him on the path to create the images that will chronicle a golden age of baseball? And from where did the vision, the talent, and the humanity come that enabled him to capture on film the soul of a 20th-century icon, the legendary Mickey Mantle?

To begin answering those questions—each of which centers on the extraordinary accomplishments of

Sweet, as a young boy in the Adirondacks, stands in front of the one-room schoolhouse he attended.

Ozzie Sweet—we must go back 80 years in time. The date was September 10, 1918, the day Oscar Cowan Corbo was born. ("I'm half-Italian, and half Swedish and Scottish," he says. "My grandparents came from the old country [Italy].")

The "Sweet" comes from his stepfather; his mother married a man named Hardy Sweet, who legally adopted young Oscar. At age 3½, Sweet moved to New Russia, New York, a small town 35 miles from Lake Placid. "We lived on a farm in the heart of the Adirondack Mountains," he says. "I was 14 years old

before we had electricity."

Growing up, Ozzie developed a love for wildlife and nature—passions that later became the focus of much of his photography. "We had chickens and pigs and sheep, and great big vegetable gardens. My mother and my Aunt Edna—my stepfather's sister—would can tomatoes and applesauce and all sorts of stuff. We had big bins of carrots and potatoes and cabbages. I remember the Depression, but we didn't feel it at all—we had so little cash anyway. My father had a machine shop along with the farm, and he was in charge of the county trucks. So that brought in more money than if we'd just had the farm."

After finishing high school, Sweet went to college at the Art Center in Los Angeles in 1938. While there, he dabbled in acting, eventually appearing in the film *Reap the Wild Wind*. He also won roles in films featuring Hopalong Cassidy and "The Duke," John Wayne.

Sweet pursued an acting career before turning to serious photography.

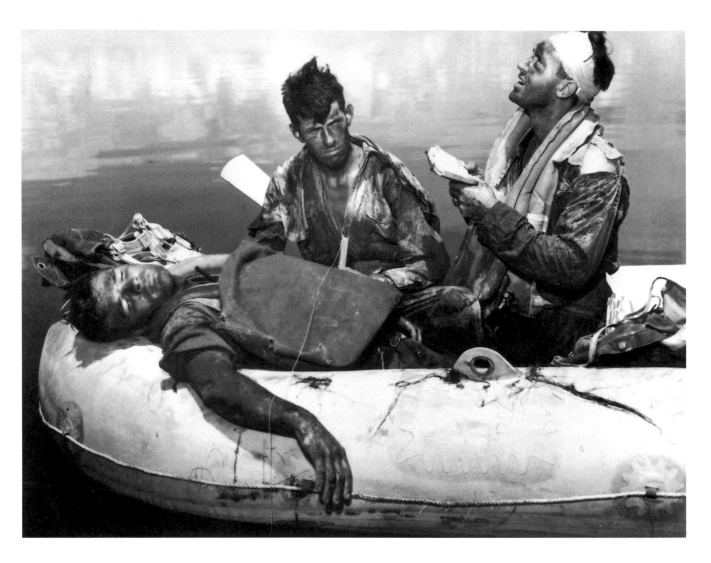

His acting career ended when he found himself drafted into the United States Army during World War II. After basic training, he became a photographer in the Signal Corp at Camp Callan near San Diego and later was commissioned as a 2nd lieutenant in the U.S. Air Force. He spent a little more

While he was in the Air Force, Sweet experimented with "simulated action" photos like the one above.

Newsweek featured Sweet's work on its covers in the late 1940s.

than five years in the service, but used the time to develop his photography talents.

A turning point came one autumn day in 1942 at Camp Callan. Sweet, using his Rolleiflex camera, began photographing his fellow soldiers during drills. One of the pictures he took that day, a black-and-white shot of an infantryman with a knife held between his teeth, ended up on the cover of *Newsweek*, marking Ozzie's debut in a national magazine. Besides the cover shot, there were several pages of Ozzie's pictures, plus text ("Train Right to Win the Fight"), inside the magazine.

During Sweet's years in the Air Force, his photos appeared on "a half-dozen more *Newsweek* covers. One of the last ones I did was my friend dressed as a Nazi soldier [see above]."

Sweet's repeat performances for *Newsweek* earned the respect of the magazine's picture editor, John Caldwell. It paid off: In 1947, as Sweet prepared to finish his tour of duty, Caldwell hired him to "concentrate on getting our covers going for us," as Ozzie recalls.

Two of Sweet's most famous subjects: geniuses Stengel and Einstein.

During the next couple of years, Sweet's subjects included Albert Einstein, Ingrid Bergman, Sean Connery, Arthur Godfrey, Bob Hope, Milton Berle, Jackie Gleason, Sammy Davis Jr., and Jimmy Durante. He also photographed such dignitaries as President Dwight David Eisenhower and Grace Kelly, the future Princess of Monaco.

One particular *Newsweek* assignment produced a remarkable twist of fate. The magazine planned a cover story on baseball's Bob Feller. Sweet came through with a simple but revealing close-up of the Cleveland Indians pitcher.

Sweet carries his bulky view camera setup during a mid-1950s assignment.

The cover caught the eye of Ed Fitzgerald, editor of *Sport* magazine, the preeminent sports publication of the day.

Fitzgerald had been anxious to contract an established photographer to give *Sport*'s covers a consistent look from month to month. "He called me and asked whether I ever had any time to shoot ballplayers—'sports personalities' to them."

Fitzgerald's timing was impeccable, for Ozzie was considering a transition from staff photographer to freelancer. He told Fitzgerald: "Yes, 'I'll have all the time in the world in about a month.' Around that time, I was quitting *Newsweek* and tackling freelance, which I've done ever since," Sweet says, smiling. "I haven't had a steady job in years!

"From then on, I visited New York just about every week for something," he adds. "*Sport* kept me busier than the dickens for years."

Sweet is not exaggerating—and his portfolio proves it. In his first year with *Sport,* 1949, he took memorable portraits of Joe DiMaggio, Casey Stengel, Lou Boudreau, Leo "The Lip" Durocher, George Mikan, Stan Musial, Don Newcombe, Jackie Robinson, and Ted Williams, among others. In 1950, his subjects included

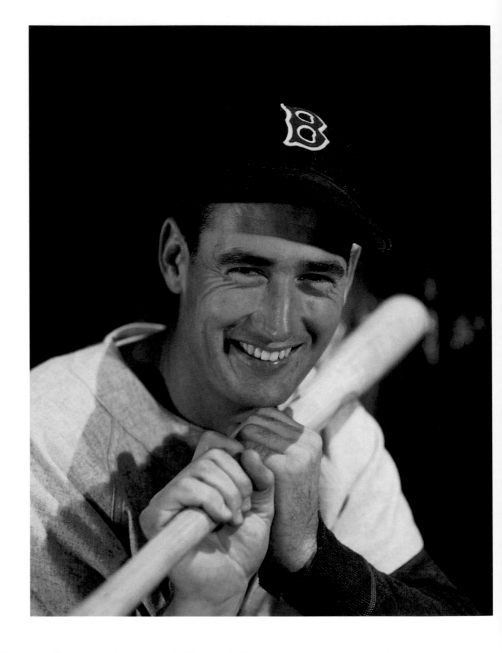

Samples of Sweet's innovative styles: Ted Williams in a stunningly sharp portrait and Jackie Robinson in a simulated action classic.

Pee Wee Reese, Joe Louis, and Ralph Branca. In 1951, it was Del Ennis, Mike Garcia, Marty Marion, and Ted Williams again. During spring training in 1952, he photographed 20-year-old Mickey Mantle, who in the years that followed would become Sweet's favorite subject. But he also continued to add to his portfolio new faces from a variety of sports.

In the early 1950s, he photographed boxer Rocky Marciano, hoop star Bob Cousy, and baseball legends Roy Campanella, Eddie Mathews, Minnie Minoso,

and Bobby Thomson. In the mid- and late-1950s, Brooklyn Dodgers heroes Carl Erskine, Gil Hodges, Pee Wee Reese, Jackie Robinson, and Duke Snider posed for Sweet. So did Larry Doby, Whitey Ford, Nellie Fox, Billy Martin, and boxer Rocky Graziano.

In the early 1960s, Sweet captured portraits of Luis Aparicio, Norm Cash, Rocky Colavito, Don Drysdale, Al Kaline, Harmon Killebrew, Roger Maris, Frank Robinson, Warren Spahn, and Maury Wills—plus football's Jim Brown, Paul Hornung, and Bobby Layne and basketball's Oscar Robertson.

In the mid-1960s, Sweet conducted several sessions with the dominant Sandy Koufax. He also photographed Hank Aaron, Tony Conigliaro, Tommy Davis, Tony Oliva, Boog Powell, and Brooks Robinson, not to mention golf's Jack Nicklaus. In the late 1960s, he shot Richie Allen, Roberto Clemente, Stan Musial, and Willie Stargell as well as hockey's Bobby Hull and Bobby Orr and golf's Lee Trevino.

Over the years, Sweet perfected a distinctive look in his photography. "My style of shooting," he says, "was 'simulated action.' And it was something Mickey Mantle did extremely well; he always turned in a great performance. He was believable."

24

Baseball's most intriguing faces—including those of Sandy Koufax and Roberto Clemente—have met up with Sweet's camera.

Ozzie's use of simulated action ploys helped him get around the fact that color film was so slow that real action close-up shots were nearly impossible.

Of course, Sweet's portfolio included more than just simulated action shots. He also specialized in breathtakingly tight portraits.

"The type of photos I got more than any other were the special close-ups," he says. "There are just so many things you can do when it comes to posing a baseball player, or a player from any sport," Sweet says. "Each year, I'd try something a little different; I'd look for a different way to see a player."

Through the years, Sweet helped set *Sport* apart. And he was as surprised as anyone that he had fallen into this line of photography. "I'll never forget: One time I was having a cover conference [at *Sport*'s offices]. And I said to Ed Fitzgerald, 'I love this. I enjoy shooting covers, and doing so many of your covers'— some years I did every *Sport* cover. 'But I don't understand it, Ed. I'm not a sports photographer.' He said, 'Ozzie, that's why we use you—because you won't cover it the usual way, the way all the other sports photographers do.'"

A variety of factors contributed to Sweet's success—mainly, planning, planning, and more planning.

Before Sweet began shooting, he would contact a team's publicist and make an appointment. "All the talking and planning took place the day before," he says. "In spring training, for example, I might shoot another subject the day before a scheduled shoot with Mickey. Then I'd spend maybe an hour getting everything together for the next morning, making sure all my equipment was right. Then I'd talk to Mickey to make sure he knew everything that was going on."

The next morning, Sweet would set up his camera on its tripod and "set his stage." Then he'd bring in the player. The actual shooting might take 15 or 20 minutes.

"Another thing I used to do—and I still do it today—is type up ideas on

Hoop legend George Mikan was one of Sweet's earlier Sport *subjects. Later, Ozzie shot football legends Jim Brown (above) and Paul Hornung.*

index cards," Sweet says. "I'd read up on the player I'd be shooting and watch him as much as I could, and take notes on a card. Then I'd put it in an acetate sleeve so it wouldn't get dirty or sloppy. That way, I'd go armed with a number of ideas I thought were suitable."

The pre-planning may sound simplistic. But, in fact, the approach was rare.

Sweet went into each session with a vision, especially for photos he knew would end up on covers. "I always dealt with covers as if they were posters," he recalls. "And a poster shouldn't have too much going on in the background."

He accomplished his clutter-free backgrounds by routinely shooting his subjects from low angles, a perspective that added a larger-than-life aura to the players.

Boston Bruins legend Bobby Orr was the focal point of this unique 1968 shot.

Another important element in Sweet's work was actually his camera. He routinely used a view camera, which gave him the truest, most honest quality possible. The view camera was one of the earliest types of camera made. Its structure allows the photographer to see in large, detailed format

28

(albeit upside-down, on a ground-glass plate at the back of the camera's body) the exact image he's about to commit to film. The larger negative format (generally 4 x 5, 5 x 7, or 8 x 10) offers the ultimate in photo quality. Most of us have seen a photographer—his head tucked under that ubiquitous black cloth attached to the top of the unit—using a view camera.

As the pictures of Sweet on pp. 1 and 21 illustrate, the view camera is large and heavy—and bulky enough that it requires the use of a sturdy tripod. It also has "swings" and "tilts" that allow the photographer to maneuver the camera in order to control a deep range of focus and perspective.

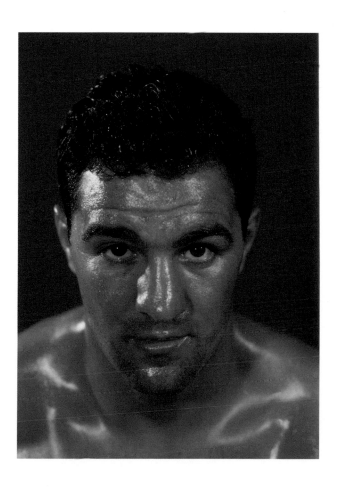

Sweet's use of a view camera—not to mention his array of props—required that he have loads of equipment with him. So when he showed up at a ballpark to carry out an assignment, he was ready to produce photos of interest. It wasn't a situation where he'd grab a camera

hanging around his neck and snap a few pictures. The view camera—which Mathew Brady used to create thousands of images during the Civil War—meant extra effort. But it paid off for Sweet, and for *Sport.*

In working with that magazine and a growing roster of other clients, Sweet operated out of New Canaan, Connecticut (for easy access to New York City) until the early 1960s. At that point, he relocated to New Hampshire. He shot regularly for *Sport* for the rest of the decade, but began cutting back as the 1970s rolled in. "It was a deliberate thing," he says. "I was a freelancer, and I wanted to do covers for as many different magazines as possible. I wanted to be a *cover expert.*"

He already was.

By that time, Sweet had created covers for *Look, Sports Afield, Field & Stream, Parade, Collier's, Ebony, Modern Photography, Family Circle, Argosy, Boy's Life, Dog World,* and *Science Illustrated,* among countless others.

As time went on, his photos showed up on the covers of *Time, The Saturday Evening Post, TV Guide, Popular Science, Popular Photography,* and *Parents.* And *Redbook, Cosmopolitan,*

Ladies' Home Journal, and Good Housekeeping. And The Sporting News, Golf, Golf Digest, Skier, Popular Boating, Ski Week, and Outdoor Life. There are many, many others.

Sweet also had the privilege of seeing his work blown up to a 60-foot-wide, 18-foot-high format—the largest picture in the world. Specifically, the sledding image above appeared as a gigantic Kodak "Colorama" (a huge transparency that was backlit) at Grand Central Station in the late 1960s. It is, naturally, a simulated action shot; the toboggan is hanging in midair, suspended from cables. A snow-

This simulated action appeared as a 60-foot-wide Kodak advertisement at Grand Central Station in the 1960s.

32

blowing machine supplies some action, while the young "actors" supply even more. Note the ski cap on the child in the rear seat; a stiff piece of wire tucked into the hat makes it look as if it's waving in the wind.

(A note on the ice-skating picture on p. 31: That's *not* simulated action. "I do not have her suspended in air with fishing leader," Ozzie points out, smiling.)

Above are simulated action shots featuring fishing and hunting scenes. At right: one of the 1,800-plus magazine covers Sweet has shot.

In the 1970s, Sweet—working with writer Jack Denton Scott—embarked on a series of award-winning wildlife and animal books. The first in the series was 1974's *Loggerhead Turtle/Survivor of the Seas* (G.P. Putnam's Sons). Others in the series include *Island of Wild Horses, The Book of the Goat, Little Dogs of the Prairie,*

Alligator, and *That Wonderful Pelican.*

To illustrate the series with some of his finest black-and-white photography, Sweet traveled extensively—to Alaska, Canada, Maine, Wyoming, the Grand Tetons, Isle Royal in Michigan, Florida, and many other sites. The treks occasionally proved dangerous. Sweet will never forget an attack in Maine by a

Sweet's photography illustrated 18 award-winning animal books in the 1970s.

mother moose "protecting" her calf; she charged Ozzie and butted him to the ground, roughing him up in the process.

As if his *Newsweek, Sport,* and wildlife book series aren't enough, Sweet has been pursuing other passions for the past 14 or 15 years. Still active at age 80, he photographs dogs and cats, fall foliage in New Hampshire, and, especially, a wide range of classic automobiles. "Cars are about 70 percent of what I do now," he says.

In photographing vintage autos, Sweet uses many of his sports techniques—elaborate settings, props, and even simulated action—to create unique imagery. On p. 36, for example, he went to great pains to set a remarkable scene: a couple riding down the road in an old Stanley Steamer, their attention turned to a deer bounding away. The models are friends of Ozzie's; the deer, of course, is mounted.

Upper right: Sweet poses in front of his 18th-century New Hampshire farmhouse.

35

Despite the incredible variety within Sweet's seemingly limitless body of work, it's his sports photography that's won the most recognition. And one of the most memorable tributes for Ozzie came from Mickey Mantle himself.

In the early 1990s, Sweet visited

Photo by Jeffrey Lowe

Ozzie Sweet poses with one of the tools of his trade. The battery of one-time-use flashes on this camera, which Sweet used for real action shots, caused a veritable "light explosion" every time he used it.

Mantle's New York restaurant. At the time, he remembers, "I hadn't seen Mickey in quite a while. But he saw me and came up to me and said, 'I gotta have my picture taken with you!' My wife Diane was there, and he insisted she pose for a photo as well. I really appreciated that."

Sweet loves the irony of the picture that resulted from their reunion—the irony of the photographer's favorite subject requesting they be shot together (see p. 12).

Not surprisingly, it remains one of his most prized possessions. And Mantle no doubt would be touched to hear Sweet tell the story today.

• • •

Today, Sweet applies his simulated action techniques during his frequent vintage automobile photographs.

Chapter 1

In the Beginning

1951–1955

Spavinaw, a tiny rural community in northeast Oklahoma, couldn't have known what it was getting on October 20, 1931, the day Mickey Charles Mantle came into the world. His father, baseball fanatic Elvin Clark "Mutt" Mantle, christened him after Mickey Cochrane, the great Philadelphia A's catcher who at the time was in the midst of a Hall of Fame career.

Four years later, the family moved to Commerce, Oklahoma, where Mickey would grow up. In his early years, young Mickey—driven by Mutt's prodding and encouragement—became a star school athlete both in baseball and in football.

During his sophomore season in high school football, Mantle suffered his first serious injury: a kick in the shin that led to a diagnosis of osteomyelitis (a chronic inflammation of the bones). At one point, the pain and swelling in Mantle's ankle became so severe that doctors actually considered amputation. Fortunately, Mantle recovered enough to resume athletics, although the problem would recur for the rest of his life.

Once he returned to sports, Mantle continued his development as an all-around star. But baseball was his passion, and he showed so much skill at the plate that in 1948, New York Yankees scout Tom Greenwade signed him to a contract. Mantle, not quite 18 at the time, prepared to play for Independence (Kansas) of the Kansas-Oklahoma-Missouri League.

Mantle had all the tools, as they say, to become a major-leaguer, and he proved it during the 1949 and '50 seasons. In his first game with Independence, "The Commerce Comet" had two hits in four at-bats and scored three runs. He hit .313 in '49, then moved to Class C Joplin (Missouri) of the Western Association in 1950. In 137 games there, he batted a league-leading .383, hitting 26 home runs and driving in 136 runs. He also led his circuit in hits (199) and runs scored (141). Unfortunately, Mantle also made 55 errors as a shortstop.

In 1952, Ozzie Sweet took his first Mickey Mantle photographs.

The following spring, in 1951, he earned a spot on the Yankees' roster as an outfielder. Early in the season, though, 19-year-old Mickey—his own toughest critic—began pressing. Manager Casey Stengel decided he needed to regain his confidence, so on July 13, he shuttled Mantle to Double-A Kansas City.

After a rough start at K.C., Mantle pulled himself together and hit .361. By August, he was back in Yankee pinstripes; he finished the '51 season with 13 homers and a .267 average. Furthermore, he won a starting spot in the World Series—in right field, next to Joe DiMaggio.

It was a bittersweet Series for Mantle. The Yankees beat the New York Giants in six games, but Mickey suffered a knee injury in Game 2 when he stepped onto a sprinkler head while pursuing a fly ball hit by Willie Mays. Mantle felt DiMaggio couldn't get to it, so he took off—only to hear Joe calling for it. Mantle tried to stop suddenly when his right shoe caught the rubber on the sprinkler head. The knee collapsed and Mantle fell—he later recounted that a piece of bone was sticking out of his leg. DiMaggio leaned over him and said, "Don't move. They're bringing a stretcher."

Despite the injury to Mantle, Stengel still predicted great things for him, and he told any reporter who would listen. As a result, "The Mick"—ready to play on his rebuilt knee—wasn't exactly a secret heading into the Yankees' 1952 camp.

Sweet's earliest Mantle images reveal the bright eyes of a star in the making.

The Minors

Regular Season

Hitting

		AVG	G	AB	R	H	RBI	2B	3B	HR
1949	Independence	.313	89	323	54	101	63	15	7	7
1950	Joplin	.383	137	519	141	199	136	30	12	26
1951	Kansas City	.361	40	166	32	60	50	9	3	11

Noteworthy

- Mantle signed his first pro contract in 1949 while sitting through a rainstorm in his car. His pay: $1,100, plus $400 for playing the remainder of the season.
- Mantle spent his first pro season at shortstop for the Yankees' Class D club at Independence, Kansas.
- Mantle stayed at shortstop the following year at Class C Joplin (Missouri), where he led the league in both runs scored and hits.
- In 1950, Pittsburgh general manager Branch Rickey offered Ralph Kiner and $500,000 for the young phenom. The Yankees refused.

That spring, *Sport* magazine sent Ozzie Sweet to St. Petersburg, Florida (the spring training home, at the time, of the world champion Yankees), to create some portraits of Mantle. Sweet remembers that first meeting vividly.

"Mickey was quiet; I don't think he said a word during those first sessions. He was barely 20, and he still had complexion problems—this was just a quiet kid from the country."

Indeed, Mantle's eyes in those early Sweet shots (pp. 40, 43, and 44) reflect a shyness and a reluctance. His baby-faced features and wide eyes reveal a player almost intimidated by the camera.

"He was practically a teenager there," Sweet says, "and he looks like it—he looks like Huck Finn. It's an interesting face, but you'll notice he couldn't come up with the great expressions he'd use later on. Look at these pictures and then look at the ones taken 15 years later, and you'll see how his face gained maturity. He really got better-looking and more appealing for the close-ups each year."

Any shyness Mantle had in front of the camera disappeared when he stepped onto a ballfield. During his first full season as a Yankee, Mantle shined, batting .311 with 23 home runs. It was a landmark year for the Yankee franchise itself, as the commemorative patch on Mantle's shoulder indicates. It reads: "1903–1952/Yankees/50th Year."

• • •

The 20-year-old Mantle, Sweet remembers, had a Huck Finn look about him.

Although Sweet took his first Mantle photos in 1952, the photographer's work with the Yankees—baseball's dominant team—began three seasons earlier, when he joined *Sport*.

That year, 1949, he photographed several personalities who would become key figures early in Mantle's career.

The first, of course, was Casey Stengel, a Mantle champion and a major factor in his development.

"The first time Casey ever saw me," Mantle said in a 1994 interview, "was in 1951—I would have been 19 years old—in Phoenix [at a training camp]. And he just kind of took me over: 'My kid.' Not 'that kid,' but 'my kid.' He'd say, 'That's my kid. We're gonna have to get him off shortstop and make an outfielder out of him.' "

Sweet's startlingly tight close-up of Stengel (p. 48) gives us an intimate look at one of baseball's most charismatic managers. Stengel's green eyes portray his warmth; the lines on his face reveal his years of wisdom; the cockeyed cap captures the personality of this colorful character.

The photo comes from a session Sweet carried out in Stengel's home. "I went to his house near New York, and brought a uniform, hat, and backdrops with me," Sweet says.

Sweet remembers Stengel as being "very cooperative and friendly." He also "was someone who took direction well," Sweet says. "He was a great actor,

Mantle In '51

Regular Season

Hitting

AVG	G	AB	R	H	RBI	2B	3B	HR	BB	SO	SB	OBA	SLG
.267	96	341	61	91	65	11	5	13	43	74	8	.349	.443

Fielding

POS-G	PO	A	E	DP	AVG
OF-86	135	4	6	1	.959

World Series

Hitting

AVG	G	AB	R	H	RBI	2B	3B	HR	BB	SO	SB	SLG
.200	2	5	1	1	0	0	0	0	2	1	0	.200

Noteworthy

- On May 1, Mantle—wearing uniform No. 6—connects for his first career home run off Chicago's Randy Gumpert.
- On July 13, Mantle is demoted to Double-A Kansas City after seeing his average sink to .261 with seven HRs and 45 RBI.
- In August, Mantle rejoins Yankees. Clubhouse manager Pete Sheehy changes his uniform number from 6 to 7.
- On October 2, in Game 2 of the World Series, Mantle's spikes get caught in a Yankee Stadium drainpipe covering while he chases a Willie Mays fly ball. Mantle misses remainder of Series.

The Yankees In 1951

Won-Lost	Finish	Manager	World Series
95-59	1st place	Casey Stengel	Defeated New York Giants, 4 games to 2.

Mantle mentor Casey Stengel supplied countless quotes for reporters of his day.

which he proved every day for the press for years. For a photographer to shoot a face like that, with the warmth and all those wrinkles, was a real treat."

At the time of the photo, 1949, Stengel was about to start his first year as the Yankees' skipper. He had managed in the National League for nine seasons between 1934 and 1943, but didn't achieve much success (a 396-742 record for the Brooklyn Dodgers and Boston Braves). That would change with the Yanks.

Beginning in '49, Stengel led the New Yorkers to five straight championships. All the while, Stengel entertained fans, players, and the press alike. Sweet caught "The Ol' Perfessor" in action on p. 47; it's an image that shows the effervescent Stengel in his natural element: holding court amidst a group of reporters. Casey's daily "park bench" spring-training sessions made him a favorite among writers looking for quotable material.

Inside the clubhouse, Stengel could be just as stern as he was entertaining outside of it.

"I'll tell you what," Mantle said. "He was *very* good with discipline. He didn't have to fine you, and he didn't have a curfew, but if he came over to talk to you, you'd better listen. When he got pissed off at me and Billy Martin or Whitey Ford, that 'Stengelese'—you know, where he talked funny, and said things that didn't make sense—didn't come into play. He'd get you in his office and he'd say, 'Listen [expletive], we're not doin' too good right now, and you'd better get

your [expletive] [expletive] into bed tonight.' Nobody ever saw that part of him. But he'd get you in his office, and he could control."

Mantle found out early that Stengel had a heart, too. He loved to tell the story about the way Casey broke the news of his 1951 demotion (from *Mickey Mantle: An American Dream Comes to Life*, written by Mantle with Lewis Early; Sagamore Press, 1996):

Two faces of Casey: in 1949 (left) and on the March 1954 Sport.

> *"We were in Detroit at the time. We had just arrived there, and I'd just had a really terrible series in Boston. Casey let me get dressed with the rest of the guys and go out on the field…. Then he sent the clubhouse man out to get me and he brought me back in. He wanted to tell me alone, by himself. Well, he had tears in his eyes, and, of course, it broke my heart. He told me, 'You've lost all your confidence. I think it would be really good for you to go down for a while. All we want you to do is just go to Kansas City and get a couple of home runs, a couple of hits, and the first thing you know, you'll get your confidence back, and we'll bring you right back up.*
>
> *"Then he said, 'You go ahead and get dressed and take off. I'll tell everybody what happened.' I always thought it was really nice of him to let everybody go out of the clubhouse before he told me."*

• • •

Among the other Yankee luminaries Sweet photographed in 1949 was Joe DiMaggio. The portrait on p. 51 captures the class and style for which "Joltin' Joe" was known. It also hints at his serious, sometimes stoic nature.

It wasn't an easy photo to take, since DiMaggio was never anxious to get in front of the camera.

"Joe was cooperative enough," Sweet says, "but he wasn't too pleasant. I'm not being critical, but frankly, he made you feel a little nervous, like he was going to walk off. He didn't make you feel comfortable. You wanted to get it done as quickly as possible.

"Years later, when Joe was going down to spring training [as a Yankee instructor], we got to be friendly," Sweet adds. "We stayed in the same hotel in St. Pete, and we got more friendly after that."

Mantle, during his stints with the Yankees in 1951, certainly felt the pressure of succeeding DiMaggio.

"When we went to spring training in Phoenix my first year [1951], I was only 19," Mantle said. "Casey Stengel started sending stories back to New York that 'We got a kid out here who's gonna be the next Babe Ruth, Lou Gehrig, and Joe DiMaggio all rolled into one. And this is Joe's last year, so Mantle will probably be our center fielder—he'll take Joe's place.'

"But, you know, you don't take Joe DiMaggio's place. That put a lot of pressure on me, and I didn't do too good my first year.

"Joe D. did leave in '52," Mickey added. "I had some fairly good years, but not anything like what Joe DiMaggio was havin'—and what Casey said I could do— until 1956. I wrote that in a book called *My Favorite Summer*, and 1956 was the reason, because I finally did what Casey said I would: win a Triple Crown. It was like it took a big boulder off my shoulders, because I finally did what he said. And it kind

"Joltin' Joe" DiMaggio's career overlapped with Mantle's in 1951. This shot dates to 1949.

of got the fans off my back about being another Joe D.: 'Joe DiMaggio my ass! You couldn't carry his glove!' I'd hear that a lot."

• • •

One of Sweet's earliest shots of Mantle features the young star kneeling in an on-deck circle (p. 53). "That's a shot a lot of photographers use," Sweet says. "You can get in close because the player's not standing. You get all of him, plus the bat. The whole thing lends itself beautifully, from the standpoint of composition, to a cover photo."

It's also a shot that, for Mantle, didn't require much direction. "That's the way Mickey would kneel—one elbow on the knee, with his bat tucked under his arm."

In fact, Mantle looks much more relaxed in this setting than in the tight close-ups taken around the same time.

• • •

The striking photo at right graced the April 1953 cover of Sport.

While Sweet spent most of the time during his annual spring training visits creating portraits and simulated action shots, he also snapped a few candids. And they often included Yankee players.

Below is an early-1950s shot of shortstop Phil Rizzuto inspecting a glove with Stengel and Gil McDougald. (It was McDougald, not Mantle, who won Rookie of the Year honors in 1951. The versatile infielder hit .306 with 14 homers, 63 RBI, and 14 steals that season.)

On p. 55, Sweet gives us a look at catcher Yogi Berra surrounded by a host of photographers in another shot that Sweet "grabbed." "I didn't stage that one," he says. "It's a spring training scene. If I had staged it, I would have chosen a place that had a cleaner background. Instead, I just grabbed it the way it was."

Both Rizzuto and Berra were longtime teammates of Mantle's. Rizzuto's career spanned from 1941–56, and his forte was defense. But he also batted .273, stole 149 bases, won an MVP award (1950), and—after years of waiting—finally earned induction into baseball's Hall of Fame in 1994.

"Scooter" Rizzuto, flanked by Gil McDougald and Casey Stengel, arrives at a mid-1950s spring training.

Throughout his career, Rizzuto served as a Yankee sparkplug. The well-liked "Scooter" also fell victim to the occasional practical joke. Mantle, in his book *The Mick* (Doubleday, 1985), related this anecdote: *"One year, Phil won an Austin-Healey sports car for being the most popular Yankee. It was real small and Phil drove*

it down to St. Pete [for spring training]. A couple of veterans grabbed ahold of the car with their bare hands and wedged it sideways between two palm trees. Phil couldn't drive it out. Still, I think he sorta appreciated the joke."

Berra played for the Yankees from 1946–1963 (he also had nine at-bats for the New York Mets in 1965). His accomplishments include a .285 career average, 358 home runs, 1,430 RBI, and three MVP awards (1951, 1954, and 1955). He also hit .274 and had 12 HRs in his 14 World Series appearances, and had his ticket punched for Cooperstown in 1971.

• • •

Tommy Henrich was another veteran star whose career overlapped—albeit briefly—with Mantle's. Nicknamed "Old Reliable," Henrich played from 1937–1950, batting .282 with 183 home runs. He was 36 when Sweet took the portrait on p. 57.

Henrich was a key Yankee for another reason. An accomplished defensive player who served as a Yankee coach in 1951, he took Mantle under his wing and showed him the subtleties of outfield play. Mantle signed with the Yankees as a shortstop, but from the beginning, Stengel felt his future was as an outfielder. So Henrich worked with him. He taught Mantle about angles and throwing, about positioning and getting a jump on the ball. During spring training in '51, Henrich hit countless fungoes to Mantle and, toward the end of camp, felt he was ready to play in the outfield in a preseason game.

In one of his first outfield appearances, an opposing batter hit a ball over Mantle's head. "The Mick" sped to the ball, caught it, and—in one motion—turned and fired a rope to home plate, preventing a runner from scoring. As legend has it, Henrich greeted Mantle in the dugout with the words, "Forget most of what I've tried to teach you about getting throws off in a hurry. That last play was a thing of beauty. Just continue to do it the way you just did."

In the 1949 portrait on p. 55, Henrich showed he could work with photographers, too. The premise of this pose, of course, is that the left-handed–hitting Henrich had just blasted a home run. As Sweet says: "He's sure making it look believable, isn't he?"

• • •

Tommy Henrich helped convert a young Mantle from infielder to outfielder.

Mantle was a natural in front of the camera, as this 1952 swing pose illustrates.

In creating his cover portraits, Sweet spent minutes that ran into hours rigging up his elaborate equipment.

"I'd bring backdrops with me all the time," he explains, "and I had a frame I'd put them into, so it would be like a studio—an outdoor portrait studio. I'd use the sunlight, but I'd also use my own fill lights to balance the lighting."

Another concern involved not Sweet's equipment or his subjects, but the distractions caused by other players who couldn't resist ribbing their teammates.

"I'd always try to get the subject back away from the dugout where the players would be hanging out," Sweet says. "If I'd set up and shoot anywhere near them, they'd come over and start making all kind of cracks. It would take three times as long. So I'd always get my subjects way off somewhere. They felt better about it, too."

• • •

Regular Season

Hitting

AVG	G	AB	R	H	RBI	2B	3B	HR	BB	SO	SB	OBA	SLG
.311	142	549	94	171	87	37	7	23	75	111	4	.394	.530

Fielding

POS-G	PO	A	E	DP	AVG
OF-141, 3B-1	348	16	14	5	.963

World Series

Hitting

AVG	G	AB	R	H	RBI	2B	3B	HR	BB	SO	SB	SLG
.345	7	29	5	10	3	1	1	2	3	4	0	.655

Noteworthy

- On May 6, Mantle's father dies of Hodgkin's disease. Mickey later says, "I'm sorry Dad really never saw me make it big."
- After playing right field as a rookie, Mantle debuts in center field on May 20 and has four hits.
- On July 26, Mantle hits first career grand slam.
- On August 11, Mantle has first multi-homer game, hitting two vs. Red Sox.
- Mantle finishes season with 37 doubles and 549 at-bats—numbers that will stand as career highs. Mantle ranks second in AL in doubles as well as slugging percentage and total bases.
- Despite a league-high 12 outfield errors, Mantle leads league in outfield double plays (five).
- On October 6, hits first World Series home run in eighth inning of Game 6. It stands up as decisive run in win over Brooklyn.
- On October 8, in Game 7 of World Series, Mantle's homer in sixth inning provides go-ahead run.
- Receives Griggs Trophy as Oklahoma Athlete of the Year.

The Yankees In 1952

Won-Lost	Finish	Manager	World Series
95-59	1st place	Casey Stengel	Defeated Brooklyn Dodgers, 4 games to 3.

Still another teammate who played a pivotal role on Mantle's early teams was pitcher Allie Reynolds. A right-hander, he began his career with the Cleveland Indians in 1942. Five years later, the Yankees acquired him for Joe Gordon and Eddie Bockman. Reynolds became a rock on the Yankees' staff, averaging 16 wins per year from 1949–54. He also won seven of his nine World Series starts.

Reynolds was known as a "protector" of his own players. Mantle felt a real kinship with Allie and the other Yankee hurlers because of the security they provided. Long before the AL adopted the designated hitter rule, a pitcher thought twice about throwing beanballs at the opposing team's stars.

"Pitchers threw at my knees if they were pissed," Mantle said. "But normally, they didn't throw at me very much, because we had Allie Reynolds and Vic Raschi. The other team's pitcher had to hit, so if I got thrown at and they knew for sure I got thrown at, that pitcher was gonna get hit the next time up.

"We didn't even have to talk to our pitchers about it. If I got hit, I'd come back to the dugout, and if Allie was pitching, he'd come over to me and nod, and I'd nod at him," Mantle added, smiling. "That's one of the things missing in the American League today."

Reynolds finished his career in New York in 1954, retiring with a total of 182 wins and a 3.30 ERA.

On the facing page is a photo in which Sweet had Reynolds and Yogi Berra feign a conference on the mound—again, simulated action. Note the seriousness in Reynolds' face as he listens to Berra's "instructions." In the 1950s, before the advent of in-your-face technologies that bring sports closer and closer to us, photographers simply couldn't get these types of close-ups during the games themselves. Hence Sweet's elaborately staged reenactments.

Allie Reynolds and Yogi Berra feign a mound conference for photographer Sweet.

• • •

The fact that Mantle was a switch-hitter actually gave photographers—and magazine designers—some options in shooting him. The photo on p. 63, in which he's hitting left-handed, comes from the same sessions as the righty-swinging shot on p. 58. Sweet directed the former, with Mantle's head in the upper left corner, with a cover in mind (although it wasn't used as one). The other is more suited for interior magazine use.

For Mantle, switch-hitting started from the time his father showed him how to swing a bat. Early in his baseball career, as a teenager back in Oklahoma, Mantle (a natural right-hander) became frustrated with his lefty results. In a game against a right-handed pitcher, when Mantle thought his father wasn't around, Mickey decided to abandon switch-hitting and stepped into the right-handed batter's box.

Unbeknownst to Mickey, his dad was in the stands. Mutt saw what his son was up to and, after the game, jumped on him for giving up. Mickey quickly resumed switch-hitting and stayed with it for the rest of his career.

• • •

Mantle In '53

Regular Season

Hitting

AVG	G	AB	R	H	RBI	2B	3B	HR	BB	SO	SB	OBA	SLG
.295	127	461	105	136	92	24	3	21	79	90	8	.398	.497

Fielding

POS-G	PO	A	E	DP	AVG
OF-121	322	10	6	2	.982

World Series

Hitting

AVG	G	AB	R	H	RBI	2B	3B	HR	BB	SO	SB	OBA	SLG
.208	6	24	3	5	7	0	0	2	3	8	0	.398	.458

Noteworthy

- On April 17 at Griffith Stadium in Washington, D.C., Mantle drives 1-0 pitch from lefty Chuck Stobbs completely out of stadium. Ball travels an estimated 565 feet and is regarded as baseball's first tape-measure blast.
- On July 6, Mantle blasts pinch-hit grand slam off Philadelphia Athletics pitcher Frank Fanovich.
- Mantle finishes third in AL in runs scored (105) and is named to the All-Star team for the first time.
- On October 1, Mantle blasts his first World Series home run at Yankee Stadium (third overall).
- Mantle continues his World Series heroics on October 4 with a grand slam at Ebbets Field.

The Yankees In 1953

Won-Lost	Finish	Manager	World Series
99-52	1st place	Casey Stengel	Defeated Brooklyn Dodgers, 4 games to 2.

The Yankees, after defeating the Brooklyn Dodgers in seven games in the 1952 World Series, began the next campaign as defending champions. Early in the '53 season, Ozzie Sweet began planning a new Mantle photo session. This one would be at Yankee Stadium, so Sweet decided to make the previous season's title a major element. He requisitioned a championship banner from the Yankees and used it as a backdrop. It was certainly apropos: Mantle had been spectacular in the '52 World Series, hitting .345 with two home runs, a triple, a double, five runs scored, and three RBI.

In Sweet's series of "banner" portraits (pp. 65–67), he managed to get some distinctly different expressions out of Mantle. It wasn't by accident, either.

"I'd ask him for a serious look," Sweet remembers. "Or he'd try a tough look [see p. 66], but he still had a baby face. Or else I'd just ask for a smile."

Ah, that classic Mantle smile.

"At that time, it still wasn't quite what it would become," Sweet observes. "Later on, of course, it was a super smile—his eyes smiled! Everything smiled. But in 1953, he was learning, which is important for a well-known personality in sports or anything else. *Develop your smile.*"

Sweet's view camera setup required the subject to remain perfectly still for a fairly long time.

"Remember, I was working with my big camera on the tripod," Sweet says. "So he had to stay put and relax. I'd get him in position, and then, in between shots, I'd tell him, 'You can relax—just don't move your feet.' Otherwise, he'd go out of focus. Then I'd have to get under that dark cloth again and get him back in focus, get it sharp. It was a lot of extra work using those big view cameras."

The payoff was in the portraits.

• • •

In 1953, Sweet posed Mantle in front of the Yanks' '52 championship banner.

Ozzie Sweet remembers how quickly his photographer/subject relationship with Mantle evolved.

"The first year [1952], he was swamped, and everyone wanted to get at him, so he did a lot of shoots. But in 1953, he did remember me from the previous spring. Of course, I don't know whether he remembered me or that bulky camera I used! I suppose it was the camera. Still, he was very, very cooperative, and he seemed more at ease than he was the first time. I think that shows in his face."

It was in 1953 that Sweet shot Mantle in a pose that would become a standard for photographers of the day (see pp. 68 and 69). Countless lensmen have captured Mantle with that familiar Yankee Stadium façade in the background, but few have done it with the precision and clarity Sweet's photos possess.

Ozzie's penchant for simulated action photography and low camera angles

Mantle enjoyed World Series exposure in each of his first three seasons.

Mantle In '54

Regular Season

Hitting

AVG	G	AB	R	H	RBI	2B	3B	HR	BB	SO	SB	OBA	SLG
.300	146	543	129	163	102	17	12	27	102	107	5	.411	.525

Fielding

POS-G		PO	A	E	DP	AVG
OF-144, SS-4, 2B-1		334	25	9	6	.976

Noteworthy

- Mantle drives in 100 runs for the first time.
- He finishes season with 12 triples—a total that will stand as his career high.
- Mantle leads AL in runs scored and places third in slugging percentage, total bases, home runs, and walks.
- Defensively, Mantle notches major-league best 20 outfield assists.

The Yankees In 1954

Won-Lost	Finish	Manager	World Series
103-51	2nd place	Casey Stengel	Did not play.

were the keys. "He looks like he's really watching the ball," Sweet says. "And it was important to have the Stadium show up.

"And notice I shoot almost everything from a lower angle," he adds. "It lends drama—you can see it in these shots [pp. 68 and 69]."

Mantle, as the detail in these photos reveals, still had a youthful appearance. "His face hadn't quite cleared up," Sweet says. "He was only 21 there—but he was already a major player on the Yankees and in the media center of the world."

The national spotlight sat well with Mantle. In 127 games in 1953, Mickey hit 21 home runs, scored 105 runs, and drove in 92. He was a main reason the Yankees returned to the World Series for the fifth year in a row.

In the Fall Classic, Mantle continued attracting the attention of baseball fans everywhere. While he hit only .208 in the Series (won by the Yankees over Brooklyn in six games), he made his hits count. Two of his five safeties were homers, and he drove in seven runs while scoring six.

Mantle was living up to Stengel's advance billing. In two-plus years in the majors, he had already played in three World Series and had four postseason home runs and 10 RBI.

• • •

Subtle details reveal that these look-alike photos are indeed different.

Bob Turley, who played with Mantle for eight years (1955–62), was an anchor in the Yankees' pitching rotation in the mid-1950s. He had several solid seasons and peaked in 1958, when he went 21-7, tossed six shutouts, had a 2.97 ERA, and won the Cy Young Award.

Pitcher Bob Turley was a teammate of Mantle's on four championship teams.

Sweet first photographed Turley in 1955, his first year in New York after a short stint with the St. Louis Browns.

The 6-foot-2, 215-pounder was "a very photogenic guy," Sweet recalls. "He didn't mind looking at the camera. While I didn't photograph him as often as I did Mantle, he knew what to do."

Note that the backdrop on the photos here is the same as those used in the Mantle photos on pp. 74–79, even though Sweet didn't shoot these the same year as the Mickey portraits. For covers, *Sport* preferred bright backgrounds, so Sweet's arsenal of backdrops always included explosive colors.

• • •

Mantle In '55

Regular Season

Hitting

AVG	G	AB	R	H	RBI	2B	3B	HR	BB	SO	SB	OBA	SLG
.306	147	517	121	158	99	25	11	37	113	97	8	.433	.611

Fielding

POS-G	PO	A	E	DP	AVG
OF-145, SS-2	376	11	2	2	.995

World Series

Hitting

AVG	G	AB	R	H	RBI	2B	3B	HR	BB	SO	SB	SLG
.200	3	10	1	2	1	0	0	1	0	2	0	.500

Noteworthy

- *On May 13, Mantle hits three home runs in one game.*
- *In All-Star Game at Milwaukee on July 12, Mantle's three-run HR ignites four-run first inning. (AL later loses in 12 innings.)*
- *Mantle finishes season with league-leading totals in home runs, walks and slugging percentage.*
- *On September 30, he hits another World Series home run, his fifth in the Fall Classic.*

The Yankees In 1955

Won-Lost	Finish	Manager	World Series
96-58	1st place	Casey Stengel	Lost to Brooklyn Dodgers, 4 games to 3.

Chapter 2

The Breakout Years

1956–1959

O zzie Sweet traveled to Florida in the spring of 1956 and made his usual photo-session appointments with the biggest stars of Major League Baseball. He would produce classic portraits of such superstars as Ted Williams, Bob Feller, and Ernie Banks, among countless others.

None of his shoots, though, would take on the significance of his Mickey Mantle sessions. This was the year, after all, that Mantle would win the Triple Crown, leading the American League in home runs, batting average, and runs batted in.

By now, the 25-year-old Mantle was looking less like the baby-faced phenom we see in Sweet's earlier portraits. He was becoming more and more comfortable in front of the camera, and his 1956 sessions (pp. 74, 76, 77, and 79) spawned some of the most intriguing portraits in Sweet's catalog. "See how he's matured there?" Ozzie says of the series. "For this particular shoot, *Sport* wanted me to concentrate on close-ups. Now that's a good smile [pp. 74 and 79], but it still doesn't compare to his smiles later on—it's still just a little tentative."

In planning this session, Sweet settled on a vibrant maroon background and planned to work a bat into each shot.

By 1956, Mickey Mantle was coming of age.

The maroon would provide *Sport*'s designers with a color that facilitated high-contrast cover lines. "Art directors used to love that," Sweet says. "None of the other photographers ever did it, and sometimes their backgrounds would get too cluttered. But this was very 'poster-y,' and that's what you do on a cover—it's a poster, really."

As for the bat, it added a natural element to the shot. But Sweet went for more than the typical batting stance, because he wanted a tight close-up.

"I wanted to get his bat and his hands in the same picture, and to keep everything tight so the magazine's art director could come in tight," Sweet says.

"It's simply a series of bat poses, because he's mighty with the bat. Give him the bat—that's the thing."

Sweet points out that the Mantle of 1956 "was beginning to get where he was more sensitive. For one of the portraits, as I remember it, I asked him to look off a little bit to his left [see p. 77] and to look concerned. I think he came through pretty well—he looks a little worried. Now, I don't know why I wanted him to look worried. But all ballplayers, when they have that much responsibility on their shoulders, are worried once in a while, don't you think?"

Note how the "concerned" shot finds Mantle looking years younger compared to the more mature-looking Mantle—snapped seconds later—on p. 79. On that one, as Sweet points out, Mantle is looking more confident, and "his eyes are starting to smile more."

Perhaps Mantle knew the type of year he'd have in 1956. That season—celebrated by Mantle himself in his 1991 book *My Favorite Summer*—marked his evolution into an all-around star. "Wonderful, isn't it?" Sweet says. "And he did it in such a short time."

Early in that 1956 season, a reporter asked Mantle about the prospect of breaking Babe Ruth's record. Mantle, who was off to a great start (he hit two home runs on opening day and had a total of 20 through the month of May),

Sweet managed to "keep it simple" while still filling the frame with several textural elements.

76

replied, "I'd rather lead the league in home runs, runs batted in, and hitting, and that's my goal for the year."

He did it, too. It was a feat that only 11 other players in the history of baseball had accomplished at the time; only two others have done it since then. Mantle won his Triple Crown by hitting 52 home runs (Vic Wertz was a distant second with 32), driving in 130 runs (Al Kaline was second with 128), and batting .353 (Ted Williams hit .345).

The latter category was close, thanks to another stellar campaign by "The Splendid Splinter." Williams and Mantle were neck-and-neck going into

the season's final series—a three-game set between, ironically, the Red Sox and Yankees. During the series, Mantle—whose Yankees had first place well in hand—got two bunt hits to help him ice the batting title.

Later, Mantle would say, "I think Ted was kind of upset about losing the title…. I remember that [reporters] asked him after it was over, 'What do you think about Mantle outhitting you?' He said, 'If I could run like him, I'd hit .400 every year!'"

For years after his retirement, Mantle would talk about how 1956 was his turnaround year. In trying to live up to Joe DiMaggio's standard during his first four seasons, Mantle felt he simply "wasn't doing it."

The fans were equally tough on him. But when you look back on the numbers, you can see how he'd been gearing up his power game. After hitting 23 home runs in 1952, he slammed 21 in 1953, 27 in 1954, and a league-leading 37 in 1955. He also had become a steady .300 hitter, posting seasons of .311, .295, .300, and .306 leading up to 1956. And he was producing runs at an increasing rate. His RBI total went from 87 in 1952 to 92, 102, and 99 in the seasons that followed.

In other words, Mantle's spectacular 1956 season didn't come out of the blue. It marked a natural progression by one of the game's "bubbling under" sluggers.

• • •

Mantle In '56

Regular Season

Hitting

AVG	G	AB	R	H	RBI	2B	3B	HR	BB	SO	SB	OBA	SLG
.353	150	533	132	188	130	22	5	52	112	99	10	.467	.705

Fielding

POS-G		PO	A	E	DP	AVG
OF-144		370	10	4	3	.990

World Series

Hitting

AVG	G	AB	R	H	RBI	2B	3B	HR	BB	SO	SB	OBA	SLG
.250	7	24	6	6	4	1	0	3	6	5	1	.467	.667

Noteworthy

- On July 10, Ted Williams and Mantle hit back-to-back HRs in All-Star Game in Washington, D.C.
- Mantle wins his first Most Valuable Player Award.
- As AL's Triple Crown Winner, Mantle leads league in home runs, RBI, and batting average. He becomes sixth AL player to earn that distinction.
- In addition to Triple Crown, Mantle also paces Junior Circuit in runs scored and slugging percentage.
- On October 8, Mantle hits home run and makes remarkable running catch in outfield to preserve Don Larsen's perfect game in World Series against Brooklyn.
- Mantle also shows up on the pop music charts after he records a song, "I Love Mickey," with Teresa Brewer.

The Yankees In 1956

Won-Lost	Finish	Manager	World Series
97-57	1st place	Casey Stengel	Defeated Brooklyn Dodgers, 4 games to 3.

At the conclusion of the Yankees' 1956 spring training, Ozzie Sweet planned a fishing excursion off Madeira Beach on the Gulf of Mexico. He hoped to bring along a few of his favorite subjects—namely, several stars from the Yankees, who worked hard during February and March in hopes of avenging their surprising World Series loss in 1955. (That season, the Yanks won their sixth American League championship in seven years. But in the '55 Fall Classic, they were upended by the underdog Brooklyn Dodgers.)

"This was around the time the Yankees were always World Series or at least American League champions," Sweet says of the spring he coordinated his fishing trip. "I spent more time with them than any other club, so I got to know them going into every season. And at the end of spring training, they always had a few days off before they went back north to play serious ball."

So near the end of camp, Ozzie extended invitations to Mantle, infielder Billy Martin, and pitchers Whitey Ford and Bob Grim.

"The last time I was on the field shooting that spring, I said to them, 'Now that you have a few days off, would you like to go deep-sea fishing? I have a friend who has a wonderful boat, and he can take us out where we can get some big ones.' They said, 'Ozzie, you bet! We'd like to!' So we set a time."

Once he had his entourage in place, Sweet took care of the boat. Actually, he didn't need to: "The boat's captain," Sweet says, "told me to come on ahead—'It won't cost you anything. If you get these guys on my boat, we won't worry about any charter fee.'"

In 1956, Sweet hosted a crew of Yankees on a memorable fishing trip.

The four Yankees on the trip weren't experienced at this type of fishing, but that only added to the challenge.

"They hadn't been deep-sea fishing—any of them, really—so they were anxious to give it a shot," Sweet says. "And before we got going, they were coached

by the boat's captain, who instructed them on how to reel in a fish."

Mantle's powerful arms wielded the fishing rod with ease.

There was one minor problem Sweet had to help solve. "We were going to be out on the water for a long time, and the players didn't have any caps with them. Whitey Ford especially got concerned that he'd get sunburnt, because he's so light-complected. So before we headed out to sea, we went to see if we could find a hat for him.

"Unfortunately, there wasn't a men's store anywhere close by, but I noticed a ladies' dress shop nearby. We headed to the shop and Whitey bought a woman's straw hat."

Ford didn't think twice about throwing fashion—and machismo—out the window in favor of comfort. As a result, he shows up in several of Sweet's fishing photos wearing rather strange headgear.

Once the crew pushed out into the water, Sweet says, "it wasn't long before [the captain] had us out where there was some real action. I think it was less than an hour after we left the dock that they were getting into some real tussles with the fish—and hauling in some big ones. Every single one of the Yankees had action, and they all hooked something. It gave me an opportunity to get some great action shots."

One of Ozzie's favorite shots from the trip is the photo of Martin reeling in a fish. "That was a pretty good-sized catch there," Sweet says. "He had a long scrap with that fish. He hooked one of the biggest ones; that's why someone on the boat gave him the towel—to help him hold on during his fight. He really

worked up a sweat. He had the best action of any of 'em."

Sweet's other personal favorite among these photos is the one of Mantle and Ford on p. 84.

"You don't even see all of Whitey, but there's something about it," Sweet says. "Those expressions are honest. Often when I'd shoot ballplayers, I'd ask for a certain expression that goes along with whatever action we're planning. But this was all very honest. That isn't acting. They're not aware of the camera. They're not carrying on or posing, they're just having fun. I had had a talk with them, and I told them I'd be shooting: 'I'll be all over the place. Just ignore me. Pretend I'm not even here.' And so they did."

While Sweet normally shot in color, he decided to use black and white on the fishing trip. "I do have a color shot of all of them," he says, "but generally, it was easier just to bang away in black and white. I was on kind of a holiday myself, so I didn't want it to seem like work. I wanted it to seem like fun.

"Usually," he adds, "I would do a lot of staging and directing—'You sit here and you stand over there; you do this, and you do that.' But there was none of that on the fishing trip. This was strictly candid. The Yankees just went ahead and did anything and everything they wanted to do, and I photographed it as it happened. Notice that none of them are looking at me in any of the pictures."

As you'd expect from pro athletes, the four Yankees actually "got a little bit competitive with each other," Sweet says. "Billy got the biggest fish, so he was crowing about it. They kidded each other quite a bit, and there was a lot of horseplay, especially between Mickey and Billy."

Sweet complemented the waves and the sun with a cooler full of chicken, soda, and beer. (Of the shots in which Mantle is "dining," Sweet says: "This is a good example of how you should eat chicken—one in each hand.")

Even on a casual fishing trip, Mantle and Ford—wearing a woman's straw hat—concentrated intently on the task at hand.

While Mickey marveled at the latest catch, Billy Martin kept his line in the water.

Between fishing and lunch, the boys on the boat had a chance to shoot the breeze. On p. 91, for example, Sweet catches Mantle entertaining Martin. "Mickey was telling some hunting story—he was holding an imaginary rifle, shooting at something. There was a lot of animation with those guys. They really enjoyed one another's company—Whitey's too. But more went on between Mickey and Billy than anyone else."

After a long day on the water, the trip wound down and the captain headed back to shore. "We didn't get back until late afternoon," Sweet recalls.

"Nothing dangerous or hazardous had happened. No one fell overboard or anything, and no one got sick. They were just relaxing."

The mood of the quartet comes through in Sweet's color picture [p. 94 and 95]. "It has a good sense of camaraderie. It's a popular picture among collectors. We've made color prints of that shot and more of them have been bought by collectors than any of my other sports photographs—partly because of the three main characters who appear in it, but also because it's so rare that you get to see well-known ballplayers of that time doing something, another sport, where they're not wearing their uniforms.

"Billy and Mickey—the way they're looking at each other—you can see

Whitey Ford managed the biggest catch of the day —or so he says.

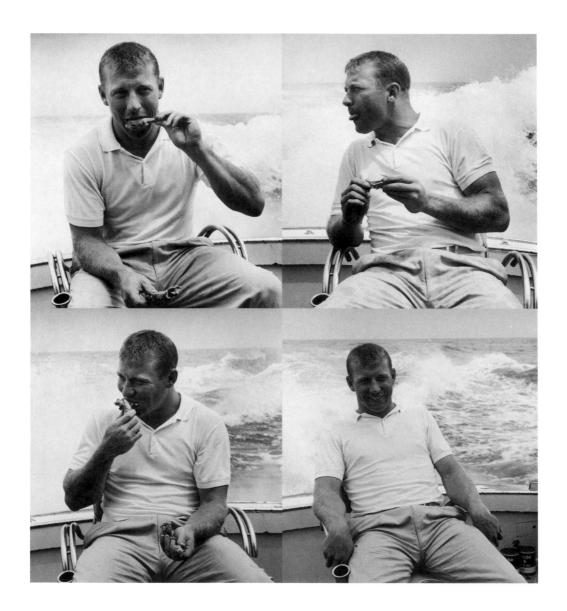

After a tasty meal of fried chicken...

they're having a helluva good time," Sweet says. "And notice Billy's holding a Coke—I made darn sure of that. We didn't bring any hard liquor—just a little bit of beer. And they drank mainly Coke."

The "other" Yankee on this trip, Grim, never achieved the notoriety his teammates did. But in the mid-1950s, he was a promising young pitcher who looked like he'd be a Yankee for years. During his Rookie of the Year season in 1954, Grim pitched in 37 games and posted a 20-6 record with a 3.26 ERA. He also became the only hurler ever to win 20 games while pitching fewer than 200 innings (he had 199). In 1955, he experienced arm troubles and posted a 7-5 record with a 4.19 ERA while pitching in both starting and relief roles.

But Grim, a Brooklynite who preferred life away from the city, loved fishing and thus was a good choice for Sweet's fishing trip. It must have relaxed him: He rebounded in 1956 to go 6-1 with a 2.77 ERA while pitching mainly as a reliever. In 1957, as a relief specialist, he posted a 12-8 record, a 2.63 ERA, and 19 saves.

By 1958, Grim's arm problems would catch up with him and he'd lose his effectiveness. Early in the '58 season, the Yankees traded him to Kansas City with outfielder Harry "Suitcase" Simpson for Virgil Trucks and Duke Maas.

During the next several seasons, Grim would end up bouncing around the bigs, pitching for Cleveland, Cincinnati, St. Louis, and Kansas City again before retiring in 1962. But his participation in Sweet's 1956 fishing trip with Mickey, Whitey, and Billy has immortalized him in a one-of-a-kind photo essay.

• • •

As his career neared its zenith, Mantle looked like he had the world by the tail.

Mickey Mantle followed up his 1956 Most Valuable Player award with a second consecutive MVP season in 1957.

While his power numbers were down a bit (34 home runs and 94 RBI in 144 games), he hit a career-high .365, stole 16 bases, and led the league in runs scored with 121. His lower home run total was due partly to the tactics of opposing pitchers; Mantle drew a league-leading 146 walks (his career high) in 1957. Meanwhile, Mantle's lofty batting average was bested only by Ted Williams, who hit .388.

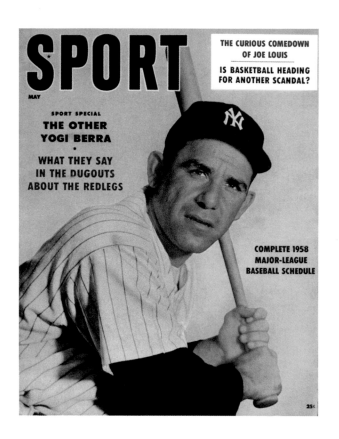

Mantle also led his team to the World Series again, although the Yankees came out as losers to Hank Aaron and the Milwaukee Braves in seven games.

The following season, 1958, Mantle continued his evolution as one of the game's most productive players. He led the AL in runs scored (127) for the third time in a row and in home runs (42) for the third time in four seasons. He also batted .300 for the sixth time in his seven full seasons. And the Yankees coasted to the American League title by 10 games over the Chicago White Sox, earning another shot at the National League champion Braves.

After four games, things looked bleak for the Yankees. They were down three games to one—and it had been 33 years since a World Series champion

Sweet captured Yogi Berra in a lighthearted moment.

recovered from such a deficit. The Yankees, though, poured it on in Games 5, 6, and 7, outscoring Milwaukee 17-5 to win the title.

By now, Mantle had won five championships in his career. Of course, he had plenty of help during this era of Yankee dominance. One of the keys to Mickey's success was Yogi Berra.

The All-Star catcher afforded Mantle protection in the batting order and—like "The Mick"—had won his own MVP awards (1951, '54, and '55). He hit at least 20 HRs every year between 1949 and 1958 and drove in 100-plus runs five times in that span. He became not only a fan favorite but a media star. Berra's own perchant for misusing the English language made him one of baseball's more quotable players. Consequently, he became a regular on magazine covers of the day. Perhaps the most appropriate Yogi portrait ever produced—for a cover or otherwise—is the one appearing here on p. 96. In it, Berra offers up a big grin while scratching his head.

Mantle In '57

Regular Season

Hitting

AVG	G	AB	R	H	RBI	2B	3B	HR	BB	SO	SB	OBA	SLG
.365	144	474	121	173	94	28	6	34	146	75	16	.515	.665

Fielding

POS-G	PO	A	E	DP	AVG
OF-139	324	6	7	1	.979

World Series

Hitting

AVG	G	AB	R	H	RBI	2B	3B	HR	BB	SO	SB	SLG
.263	6	19	3	5	2	0	0	1	3	1	0	.421

Noteworthy

- After his Triple Crown season in 1956, Mantle's contract more than doubles, to $65,000. "It was more money that I thought existed," Mantle would say later. "It was almost too much."
- On July 23, in game against Chicago White Sox, Mantle hits for the cycle.
- Mantle leads the league in runs scored and walks.
- Wins second consecutive MVP Award.

The Yankees In 1957

Won/Lost	Finish	Manager	World Series
98-56	1st place	Casey Stengel	Lost to Milwaukee Braves, 4 games to 3.

"He used to do that all the time," Sweet says. "He used to take off his hat and, with the cap in his hand, scratch his head."

In recalling that shot, Sweet says, "everything was arranged ahead of time. *Sport* wanted a close-up. They said, 'Get right up there. We wanna see that face. We wanna see the gap in his teeth. We wanna see all the wrinkles. We wanna see that guy.' And Yogi was great; he was very cooperative."

In fact, Sweet recalls, "There's a little story about this one that's kind of nice. I had the backdrop and reflectors and lights and everything set up fairly close to the dugout—I couldn't get far enough away. His teammates started coming up and laughing about how everything was staged. They weren't insulting him, but they were kidding him—they used to pick on him a little anyway. And you know what he said? 'Leave Ozzie alone! He knows what he's doing!'"

Sweet appreciated the defense—and went on to capture a fittingly characteristic shot of one of baseball's more memorable personalities.

On the other hand, there's the proverbial "one that got away." Sweet still regrets one Berra photo he didn't get—a shot he planned to take of Yogi, not exactly the most outgoing player, with a group of attractive models.

"I asked Yogi to pose with all these pretty girls I brought to spring training one year and he said, 'Ozzie, I won't do that. I've got a wife, and she'd kill me.' So I picked another player. But Yogi was the one I wanted with all the models."

• • •

Early in the 1957 season, *Sport* magazine sent Sweet to Yankee Stadium to photograph Mickey Mantle with two of his "partners in crime," Billy Martin and Whitey Ford. In one of the pictures (p. 103), Sweet staged the three of them to look as if they were plotting and scheming another of the off-the-field, late-night escapades for which they'd become infamous. He also took some straightforward group portraits, one of which appears above. Sweet still refers to this group of photos as his "Bad Boys" shots.

"The reason I photographed the three of them together is because they had that little bit of 'difficulty' in a bar," Sweet explains, referring to a brawl at New York's Copacabana nightclub on May 16, 1957, Martin's birthday. The incident allegedly involved Martin and some locals. The Yankees who were out that

Ford, Mantle, and Martin were the ringleaders for many of the Yankees' hijinks.

night—Mantle, Martin, and Ford as well as Berra, Hank Bauer, and Johnny Kucks—insisted none of them were involved in the fight.

"They did get a lot of notoriety for their antics, so the editors of *Sport* asked me to get some pictures of the three of them," Sweet says. "I took two portraits of them posing together—the 'Three Musketeers' kind of thing. And for the other one, shot with a smaller camera, I had them putting their heads together: 'What are they hatching up now?'

"I picked a place where I could get one of the guys down lower, so they weren't all in a line," Sweet continues. "And, of course, I had Billy look like he's the instigator—because the feeling was that he was the instigator. Whitey and Mickey were listening; they're giving him their complete attention: 'Yeah? Yeah?' And that's really the way it was. At least, that's the way it seemed. That's why Billy didn't last much longer with the Yankees."

Roughly a month after the Copacabana episode, during a beaning incident in a game against the Cleveland Indians, Martin threw a flurry of punches at Larry Doby. For the Yankee brass, it was the last straw. The team didn't waste

Regular Season

Hitting

AVG	G	AB	R	H	RBI	2B	3B	HR	BB	SO	SB	OBA	SLG
.304	150	519	127	158	97	21	1	42	129	120	18	.445	.592

Fielding

POS-G	PO	A	E	DP	AVG
OF-150	331	5	8	2	.977

World Series

Hitting

AVG	G	AB	R	H	RBI	2B	3B	HR	BB	SO	SB	SLG
.250	7	24	4	6	4	1	0	3	7	4	1	.583

Noteworthy

• *Mantle leads AL in runs scored, home runs, and walks.*

The Yankees In 1958

Won-Lost	Finish	Manager	World Series
92-62	1st place	Casey Stengel	Defeated Milwaukee Braves, 4 games to 3.

any time in shipping him off to Kansas City. "It was Billy," Sweet says, "who took the brunt of the thing."

For Mantle, losing Billy was difficult. "We were like brothers," Mantle later said. "When they traded him, it was the same as if one of my own brothers had been sent away."

Billy Martin's stay with the Kansas City Athletics didn't last long. He finished out the 1957 season with K.C. but was moved to Detroit in a 13-player trade in November.

The following spring, in 1958, Sweet captured Martin in a Tigers uniform for a *Sport* cover. Martin had never put up big numbers; between 1950 and 1957, he had 39 home runs, 215 RBI, and 26 steals. His best season was 1953, when he had 15 homers and 72 RBI to go with a .257 average. But the high visibility he got during his Yankee years made him an appealing cover choice—the way basketball's Dennis Rodman became a frequent cover boy on sports magazines in the 1990s.

Because Martin was known more as an intelligent, fundamentally and defensively sound player, Sweet shot him posed not with a bat but with a glove (p. 105). Martin, in Sweet's portrait, looks very much like the field general he was. "I had him put his hands up, as if he were shouting signals from second base," Sweet recalls.

Ozzie remembers the feisty Martin as someone who was pleasant to be around. "And," Sweet points out, smiling, "he had nice teeth. That's something a photographer always notices."

Martin also looked striking in a Tiger uniform—but he didn't stay in Detroit long, either. After hitting .251 with 10 homers in 1958, he found himself traded to Cleveland, where he became a part-time player in '59. (He stayed there for one season before getting traded across state to Cincinnati. The Reds kept him one

Sweet captured the three "partners in crime" plotting another prank.

season, then moved him to Milwaukee in 1961. Two months into that season, the Braves moved him to Minnesota. It would be Billy's last year in the majors.)

Meanwhile, Mantle closed out the 1950s with a subpar season—for him. In 144 games in 1959, he hit .285 with just 75 RBI while striking out a career-high 126 times. The Yankees were equally subpar: a 79-75 record and a third-place finish.

Mantle did manage to hit 31 home runs in '59, giving him 280 career blasts in just under nine seasons. Even so, the Yankees' general manager, George Weiss, sent Mickey his 1960 contract with a $17,000 pay cut. Mantle held out briefly, but ended up showing up in camp and agreeing to just a $10,000 pay cut, from $72,000 to $62,000.

The fun ended when the Yankees traded Martin to the Kansas City A's, who later traded him to Detroit.

Mantle In '59

Regular Season

Hitting

AVG	G	AB	R	H	RBI	2B	3B	HR	BB	SO	SB	OBA	SLG
.285	144	541	104	154	75	23	4	31	94	126	21	.392	.514

Fielding

POS-G	PO	A	E	DP	AVG
OF-143	366	7	2	3	.995

Noteworthy

- *On June 22, Mantle hits two home runs and a triple, drives in six runs, and scores three times in 11-6 win at Kansas City.*
- *Mantle leads AL outfielders in fielding percentage.*
- *He also reaches a career high in stolen bases, finishing second in the American League.*

The Yankees In 1959

Won-Lost	Finish	Manager	World Series
79-75	3rd place	Casey Stengel	Did not play.

Chapter 3

Glory
Days

1960–1964

One particular Mickey Mantle photo session stands out in Ozzie Sweet's mind more than any other. It happened during the dawn of the new decade, and it involved two human "props"—an umpire and a catcher. Sweet set out to achieve a "pitcher's-eye" view of Mantle, with No. 7 standing at the plate and, in some variations, following through with his sweet swing.

"I wanted to get a certain feeling with this one," Ozzie recalls. "It was a staged shot; he was waiting at the plate, and I wanted a catcher and an umpire in the background. It was a low-angle shot that we did early one morning at spring training.

"Pulling it all together—the preliminary arrangements—took at least a couple of hours, but the actual photography took 20 minutes. And the whole session wouldn't have been worth a damn without

Mickey's expression. He'd have the look, and the eye, and he'd make it appear as if he were really focused on the ball. And then he'd swing and his eyes would follow what would be the ball jumping off the bat.

"He was a performer, an actor, and he could make the photos believable."

The session took place before the 1960 season. "It would have been a little harder to pull it off after the season started up north," Sweet says. "The time to do it was down in Florida. So the day before, I talked to Casey Stengel and the

Sweet used "actors" to fill out these simulated action shots.

Mantle excelled at feigning the action.

Yankees' different coaches, and I arranged everything with a real umpire and a catcher. The guys all came out early to do this shoot, before everything got going on the field.

"The catcher had to look like he was on another team," Sweet points out. "Notice he has red sleeves: That may not seem like an important detail, but it took some planning. It's a good example of why a photographer shouldn't just come to the field and say, 'I wanna shoot this.' There's no way in the world you can pull it all together without advance notice."

While Sweet brought with him a photography assistant to pitch in with the setup, he also got help from another source: Mantle himself.

"By that time, I'd photographed Mickey so many times that he was quick to cooperate," Sweet says. "He even helped me get [the catcher and the umpire] by telling them, 'Ozzie's a good guy. Do your best for him.'"

In executing the shoot, Sweet used a few of his own trademark touches: "Again, see that I'm shooting low. Notice you don't see any tropical foliage—no palm trees, just clouds. It's got to look like it was taken anywhere. I took a couple of shots of Mickey cocked and waiting for the pitch, and then a couple of him as though he'd just hit it. Mantle, the catcher, and the umpire all had to be looking in the exact same direction, which took a certain amount of directing."

Mantle's "performance," as Sweet likes to call it, included a variety of distinctive facial expressions. In one, on p. 110, he looks All-American. Compare it to the similar pose on p. 108, where he looks more intense.

"I like the whole feeling of that one," Sweet says. "He looks like the menacing home run hitter, and the photo has good and rich flesh tones. Everything about it is good."

By 1960, Mantle's injuries left him in consistent pain. Besides the serious knee injury he incurred during the 1951 World Series, he had suffered a rash of other ailments:

- a reinjured right knee requiring an operation in 1952;

- an operation to remove a cyst behind his right knee in 1954;

- a sprained left knee in 1955;

- a pulled right thigh muscle in 1955 (which he would reinjure in 1962);

- a right shoulder injury in 1957; and

- a fractured right index finger in 1959.

There would be more to come.

"Mickey didn't talk about the injuries much," Sweet says. "But I can remember seeing him swinging and seeing the pain on his face as he twisted."

Mantle had become accustomed to playing in pain, and he proved it during the 1960 season. He played in a career-high 153 games, and his 40 home runs and 119 runs led the American League.

Plus, he had a new slugging partner in the Yankees' lineup: Roger Maris. Acquired from the Kansas City Athletics in December 1959 with two other players for Hank Bauer, Don Larsen, Norm Siebern, and Marv Throneberry, the 26-year-old Maris blossomed in 1960. He hit 39 home runs, drove in 112 runs, and won the AL MVP award, edging Mantle by three points.

The exploits of Mantle and Maris paved the way for the Yankees' return to prominence. The team went 97-57 in 1960 and met the underdog Pittsburgh Pirates in the World Series. Picking up where they left off in the regular season, the Yanks outhit the Pirates, 91-60, and outscored them, 55-27, in the seven games.

If not for Bill Mazeroski's bottom-of-the-9th home run off Ralph Terry in Game 7, the Yanks would have won their third title in five years.

Today, of course, baseball fans remember the 1960 World Series for its shocking ending. Almost lost in the drama was the fact that "The Mick" had his finest Fall Classic ever, batting .400, compiling a slugging average of .800, driving in 11 runs while scoring eight, and blasting three home runs.

• • •

Regular Season

Hitting

AVG	G	AB	R	H	RBI	2B	3B	HR	BB	SO	SB	OBA	SLG
.275	153	527	119	145	94	17	6	40	111	125	14	.402	.558

Fielding

POS-G	PO	A	E	DP	AVG
OF-150	326	9	3	1	.991

World Series

Hitting

AVG	G	AB	R	H	RBI	2B	3B	HR	BB	SO	SB	SLG
.400	7	25	8	10	11	1	0	3	8	9	0	.800

Noteworthy

- On July 4 against the Washington Senators, Mantle hits the 300th home run of his career.
- Mantle led the American League in both home runs and runs scored.
- Mantle turned in one of the better World Series performances of his career, batting .400 with three home runs as the Yankees lost to Pittsburgh.

The Yankees In 1960

Won-Lost	Finish	Manager	World Series
97-57	1st place	Casey Stengel	Lost to Pittsburgh Pirates, 4 games to 3.

Mantle In '60

Roger Maris' MVP performance in 1960 put him on the map in the world of sports. As such, *Sport* sent Ozzie Sweet to capture the lefty-hitting outfielder on film during the season, and the photographer returned with his inimitable "classic slugger pose" shots. On p. 114, the snapped-from-below angle—with the familiar Yankee Stadium façade in the background—offers remarkable detail, from the texture of the Yankee pinstripes to the blue-green color of Maris' eyes to his name (written in black marker) on the knob of his bat.

In a companion shot from the same session (p. 121), Sweet captured Maris leaning on his bat, with his trademark short-cut sleeves showing off his less-than-beefy (at least by today's standards) forearms and biceps. Sweet's fine focus caught every droplet of sweat glistening on Maris' face, neck, and arms.

These photos offer a more stunningly close look at Maris than any others taken in the era.

Earlier that year, Sweet photographed Maris in spring training. Two of those images appear on pp. 116 and 117. In one, Sweet used several bats in the foreground to frame Maris' face. The portrait depicts Roger—a season away from the pressures of chasing Babe Ruth's home run record—looking very relaxed. (Note the lighter complexion compared to Sweet's midseason Yankee Stadium shots, a telltale sign that it's spring training photography.)

In the shot on p. 117, Sweet utilized his "Yogi Berra pose"—a tight shot of Maris scratching his head, cap in hand. This portrait would appear as *Sport*'s cover in February 1962.

Ironically, Maris' presence on the Yankees helped to absorb the boos of Yankee Stadium fans—boos that in the past were usually reserved for Mantle. "The Mick," despite his stellar play, had been treated inconsistently by the tough New York fans, who weren't exactly patient with strikeouts, slumps, and

The Yankee Stadium façade provided an ideal backdrop for Sweet's portraits of Yankee heroes like Maris.

the occasional tantrum Mantle threw earlier in his career.

For Mantle, the tide started to turn in the 1960 season. In an August game that year, with Maris on first, Mantle hit a ground ball and failed to run it out. Maris hurt himself in an (unsuccessful) attempt to break up the double play. When Mantle got thrown out at first, the fans let him hear it.

Mantle heard even louder boos the following night during player introductions. But he quickly silenced the jeers by hitting two home runs in an important Yankee win. From then on, New York started to appreciate his presence—especially in light of his insistence on playing through pain.

• • •

Smiles were rare from Maris, who felt tremendous pressure during his 1961 home run chase.

Over time, as Mantle continued winning over Yankee fans, Ozzie Sweet was there to capture his maturing. Mickey, as usual, offered his full cooperation. "By then, he was helping an old buddy," Sweet says. "And he was wanting to behave properly as much as I was."

Evidence of their cohesiveness shows up in a pair of 1960 spring training pictures that depict the most relaxed Mantle you'll see this side of Sweet's 1956 fishing trip photos.

Maris (left) and Mantle were
1-2 in the MVP voting in
1960 and 1961.

The "M&M Boys" combined for 115 home runs in 1961.

The image on p. 119, which takes on the feel of a candid shot, reflects Mantle's All-American looks in a straight-on portrait. "It's just good old casual stuff," Sweet says. "I like it because there's nothing else taken of him with that look.

"And," Sweet says of the companion shot, p. 120, "look at his shoulders, and his big, thick, powerful neck. They give you a feeling of his power, and of what he

could do with that bat in his hands."

Maris, by contrast, didn't have the imposing physique Mantle had, as Sweet's "swing series" on pp. 122 and 123 illustrates. But he had everything else going for him in the early 1960s: bat speed, the short right-field porch in Yankee Stadium (a haven for left-handed power hitters), and Mickey Mantle hitting behind him.

Sweet captured Maris' fabled swing at every instant.

If Mantle and Maris were tough on pitchers in 1960, they would get downright brutal in 1961.

• • •

Baseball fans knew the Yankees' batting order of the 1920s as "Murderers' Row," thanks to the nonstop power barrage provided by Babe Ruth, Lou Gehrig, Tony Lazzeri, Bob Meusel, and others. But that outfit had nothing on the relentless '61 Yanks, a team that ultimately would set an all-time home run mark (240, a record that stood until 1996, when the Orioles hit 257) while posting a 109-53 record.

At the helm in 1961 was first-year manager Ralph Houk. In a classic case of age discrimination, Stengel had been forced out after the 1960 season because management felt he was too old. (At the press conference announcing his "retirement," Stengel said, "I guess this means they fired me. I'll never make the mistake of being 70 again.")

Even so, Houk was a logical successor who had already earned his (pin)stripes. "The Major" served as either a coach under Stengel or a minor league manager in the Yankees' farm system from 1953–1960. For years, the team had groomed him to carry on the franchise's winning legacy.

In 1961, it certainly helped Houk that he could pencil "The M&M Boys," Mantle and Maris, into the heart of his batting order. They had plenty of support, too, from singles hitters Bobby Richardson and Tony Kubek plus Bill "Moose" Skowron, Elston Howard, Clete Boyer, and Yogi Berra.

For Maris, the 1961 season started slowly—he hit just one home run in April (Mantle had seven). But he erupted for 11 in May, and between June 2 and 22, he blasted 15 homers to raise his total to 27.

As Maris stalked Ruth's record of 60, so too did Mantle; "The Mick" had 33 homers by July 19. That was the day commissioner Ford Frick (Ruth's one-time ghostwriter) announced that if a player were to break Babe's record, he'd need to do so in 154 games, since each team's schedule increased in 1961 from 154 games to 162. If someone needed the whole season to break Babe's record, the new total would carry a "distinguishing mark" in baseball's official statistics.

Despite the politics, Mantle and Maris kept blasting away. Roger, after ripping 13 homers in July and 11 in August, reached September with 51. Mantle hit 14 in July and nine in August to give him 48 on September 1.

Unfortunately, an aching shoulder, a pulled forearm muscle, and a serious

hip infection slowed Mantle during the home stretch, and he fell off the pace. He finished with 54 homers. Maris, of course, went on to hit 61 and become the new single-season home run leader—asterisk and all. (Mantle watched Maris' final two home runs that year from a hospital bed, where he was recovering from the hip infection.) Between them, Mantle and Maris set a record for most home runs by two teammates, breaking by eight the total Ruth and Lou Gehrig put up in 1927 (the year Babe hit 60 homers).

Mantle shared the Yankee Stadium spotlight with Roger Maris in 1961.

Later, Mantle talked about how much he enjoyed the home run chase. Conversely, the pressure on Maris was intense. The press hounded him, and the fans weren't unanimously rooting for him as he approached the mark of America's ultimate sports icon.

"Not many people are prepared for a fame this intense, and it came almost overnight to Roger," Mantle wrote in *All My Octobers* (HarperCollins, 1994). "No player ever accomplished so much and enjoyed it so little. As he closed in on the record, the buildup engulfed him.... I think Maris was resented because he had the irreverence to attack the record of baseball's greatest hero, but he had none of the gaudy color that the fans had come to expect of their idols."

Just the same, Maris was a hot commodity for sports magazines. During the 1961 season, Ozzie Sweet went to Yankee Stadium to create portraits of Mantle and Maris face to face, back to back, and straight-on. In the pictures, they "look like buddies," Sweet notes, referring to the media's attempt to create animosity between Mantle and Maris. Again, from *All My Octobers:* "One thing the home run duel didn't cause was a problem on the team or in the clubhouse," wrote Mantle, who actually shared an apartment with Maris.

(An interesting note on these shots: For its May 1963 issue, *Sport* needed a picture of Berra with Mantle. Lacking a cover-quality choice, the magazine recycled one of these Mantle/Maris images and replaced Roger's face with Yogi's. That cover appears on p. 128.)

In contrast to Sweet's harmonious working relationship with Mantle, the photographer didn't have a history of shooting Maris, so their 1960 and '61 sessions were challenging. "He was quiet," Sweet recalls. "I don't think he said two words at any time I was ever with him. He was very cooperative, just very quiet.

Despite rumors to the contrary, Mantle and Maris got along throughout the home run chase.

Mantle In '61

Regular Season

Hitting

AVG	G	AB	R	H	RBI	2B	3B	HR	BB	SO	SB	OBA	SLG
.317	153	514	132	163	128	16	6	54	126	112	12	.452	.687

Fielding

POS-G	PO	A	E	DP	AVG
OF-150	351	6	4	0	.983

World Series

Hitting

AVG	G	AB	R	H	RBI	2B	3B	HR	BB	SO	SB	SLG
.167	2	6	0	1	0	0	0	0	0	2	0	.167

Noteworthy

- *Mantle battled Roger Maris throughout the summer in pursuit of Babe Ruth's single-season home run record.*
- *In addition to finishing second to Maris in homers, Mantle led the AL in walks and slugging percentage.*
- *Mantle's season ended early, as he entered the hospital on September 29 with a hip infection.*

The Yankees In 1961

Won-Lost	Finish	Manager	World Series
109-53	1st place	Ralph Houk	Defeated Cincinnati Reds, 4 games to 1.

When we'd finish a shoot, I'd thank him and shake his hand, and he'd just smile."

The most famous Sweet/Maris concoction is the "flying bats" photo on p. 130. That shoot involved an intricate setup featuring several bats arranged to look as though they had been flung into the air by Maris.

"We had to come with a frame," Sweet explains of the setup he and his assistant, Nick Scutti, rigged up. "I had light stands that extended up [several feet], plus a crossbar—from which the bats would hang—about eight feet overhead."

Sweet used fishing line to hang the bats off the crossbar. "Can you imagine how much time it took to adjust the bats and get 'em just the way we wanted 'em? It took about two hours to hang them just so, to get that effect, to get the feeling, to get the camera in place," he recalls.

"I had a place for Maris, and Nick was about his height, so he acted as a stand-in.

"I had alerted Roger the day before the shoot and told him what we were going to do," Sweet adds. "Of course when he saw it, he couldn't help but smile—he really got a kick out of it."

The "flying bats" concept was Sweet's; he had been searching for a unique way to depict a slugger.

"Here was another guy who was mighty with the bat," he says. "I thought,

Maris appears with Mantle in the photo at right, but his face was replaced by Yogi Berra's in an alternate shot used on the May 1963 cover of Sport.

'I've gotta do something [to reflect that].' Usually, you get a hitter waiting for the pitch, or swinging. But Maris was so hot that I wanted to do something special with him. And I dreamed that one up.

"It was a lot of work, but it sure was fun. And the lighting was so good.... That's another thing—you pick the time of the day that you get cross light. Instead of a front light on the bats, they have some contour, and you see them so much better."

The result: "One of my favorites among all my baseball shots," Sweet says.

• • •

The Yankees rode their record-breaking power into the 1961 World Series, where they beat the Cincinnati Reds in five games. In the team's first championship since 1958, it wasn't Maris (two hits in 19 at-bats) or an injured Mantle (one hit in six at-bats in two games) who led the way. It was the performance of such unheralded contributors as Bill Skowron (.353 in the World Series); Bobby Richardson (.391 Series average); and Johnny Blanchard (two homers and a .400 Series average). Even more important was the pitching of Edward "Whitey" Ford.

Sweet's elaborate preparation was especially evident in this photo of Maris "throwing" a handful of bats.

Nicknamed "The Chairman of the Board," Ford had a spectacular Series, pitching a two-hit shutout in Game 1 and teaming up with Jim Coates on a five-hit shutout in Game 4. Two games, two wins, 14 innings, a perfect 0.00 ERA. Plus, he ran his string of scoreless World Series innings to 32, breaking a record set by Ruth when he pitched for the Boston Red Sox.

Ford's brilliance didn't surprise anyone. While the Yankees' offense battered opponents in 1961, Ford was almost an automatic win every time out. In 39 starts, he posted a 25-4 record with 209 strikeouts in 283 innings.

And as the Yankees' ace, Ford was an obvious choice as a Sweet photo subject. In the 1961 session represented here, Ozzie took different approaches on similar shots.

Of the photo at right, Sweet says: "You can see I'm shooting Whitey from above, which is unusual. He's [peering] toward the catcher as if he's trying to get a signal. And see how it shows his hand with the ball? It's a completely different angle. This part of the [windup] brings the ball, his glove, everything into the picture, and you can still come in tight."

In setting up this photo, Sweet stood on a stepladder. His assistant steadied the ladder and the camera, which was held in place with bungee cords.

In the photo on p. 133, Sweet used his patented ball-on-fishing-leader-line tactic. "The ball is out of focus deliberately," Sweet says, "because it makes it look like the action isn't stopped. The ball appears blurred because of the 'action.'"

Sweet got the effect simply by giving the ball a little push just before tripping the shutter.

Unlike the overhead view of Ford on p. 132, Sweet took his more usual angle

By changing angles, Sweet provides different views of Yankee ace Whitey Ford.

from underneath on this one. He did it by putting his subject on a door—which was propped up horizontally onto two wooden sawhorses a few feet off the ground. Then he'd spread infield dirt on the door to create the illusion of a pitcher's mound. "Yes, that's artificial height," Ozzie says, "or otherwise, I would have had to scrunch right down into the ground, and I'd get trees and stuff in the background."

• • •

Mickey Mantle began his career in the shadow of the great "Yankee Clipper," Joe DiMaggio, but by the early 1960s, he'd become a legend in his own right. And because DiMaggio regularly attended the Yankees' spring training camps as a special instructor, as well as Old-Timers' Day games and other special events, it wasn't unusual for photographers to grab a shot or two of the center fielders together.

In 1961, Sweet arranged to get Mickey and Joe together for a session. The fruits of what turned out to be a "quickie" shoot are represented on pp. 135 and 136, and they go a long way in capturing the pair's personalities.

Mantle, familiar with Sweet's work and knack for directing a shoot, looks relaxed and confident. DiMaggio, who never enjoyed posing or posturing, looks antsy and uncomfortable. Because of DiMaggio's reluctance, Sweet treaded lightly, working as efficiently as he could in order to get finished. "With anyone else, I might say, 'Adjust your cap....' But with Joe, I didn't dare," he says. "I just wanted to quickly get some images of the two of them together."

Of the few pictures Sweet took, the one on p. 135 is most enduring. DiMaggio at least *tries* to look comfortable, while "The Mick" flashes his appealing smile. On the other hand, the shot on p. 136 is more of an outtake, mainly because DiMaggio is straining his neck in an effort to move his head closer to Mantle's. "I didn't know what the heck he was doing there," Sweet says. "But with Joe, I didn't want to fool around for long. I didn't want to say, 'Mr. DiMaggio, could you please change the angle of your neck so you don't look like a turtle?' I think he might have walked away!"

Sweet is characteristically understanding in recalling the session. "Think of all the years Joe had been around by that time," Sweet points out, "and how often he'd worked with the press.

"Actually," he adds, "the way I'd word it would be: 'put up with the press.' He wasn't rude or anything, and as a photographer you could tell in a second he was harmless. But you also knew he'd rather not be doing it. And I think as time went on, he started to feel even stronger about not doing it. That was something we talked about."

• • •

Occasionally, Sweet put down his bulky view camera and snapped casual pictures of various ballplayers, including Mantle. The trio of early-1960s candids presented on pp. 137, 138, and 139 finds "The Mick" taking it easy in a natural element for him: the dugout. In one memorable shot (facing page), he beats the heat with a towel draped over his head, unconcerned with the presence of a photographer. Note Whitey Ford in the foreground. In another (p. 139), he shares a laugh with a pair of Yankee batboys.

In a third shot (p. 138), Mantle smiles directly at Sweet's camera and

Not all of Sweet's best Mantle portraits were posed.

reveals a hint of cockiness mixed with an air of contentedness. The picture preserves the boyish look of a legend, a hero who had already earned his place in baseball lore. This candid, unlike Sweet's carefully staged color portraits, is a spur-of-the-moment grab that captures the mood of a breezy summer day at the ballpark. The use of black-and-white film adds a vintage feel to an exceptionally warm photo of Mantle.

Relaxing in the dugout, Mantle has the confident air of a man at the top of his profession.

• • •

Regular Season

Hitting

AVG	G	AB	R	H	RBI	2B	3B	HR	BB	SO	SB	OBA	SLG
.321	123	377	96	121	89	15	1	30	122	78	9	.488	.605

Fielding

POS-G	PO	A	E	DP	AVG
OF-117	214	4	5	1	.978

World Series

Hitting

AVG	G	AB	R	H	RBI	2B	3B	HR	BB	SO	SB	SLG
.120	7	25	2	3	0	1	0	0	4	5	2	.160

Noteworthy

• In May, Mantle is hospitalized with a torn thigh muscle. But he returns quickly and captures his third MVP Award.
• Mantle leads the league in walks and slugging percentage.
• Mantle also wins his only Gold Glove Award.

The Yankees In 1962

Won-Lost	Finish	Manager	World Series
96-66	1st place	Ralph Houk	Defeated San Francisco Giants, 4 games to 3.

Entering the 1962 season, the Yankees were atop the baseball world. They were again the defending champs, they still boasted baseball's most potent line-up, and they still had the drawing power of Mickey Mantle and Roger Maris. Despite the latter's record-breaking performance in 1961, Sweet's first priority in 1962 was to capture more Mantle portraits.

The result: some close-ups of "The Mick" set against a bright yellow back-drop. (Sweet would use the same backdrop for a 1965 session, as presented on pp. 171–173).

One of the yellow-backed 1962 shots was a straight-on, no-frills look at Mantle (opposite). *Sport* actually held this shot for three years; it appeared as a full-page picture inside the August 1965 issue.

The 1962 session did, however, spawn a cover shot that *Sport* used right away: a profile of Mantle in which he's looking to his right (p. 143).

But the most creative shot from this session finds Mantle in another of his natural elements: autographing a baseball for a flock of young fans (p. 142). Sweet directed the boys in this "simulated-signing" photo to look giddy and excited about meeting Mantle—which probably wasn't difficult for the star-struck young fans. This unique photograph has a sort of Rockwellian feel: It boasts the same wide-eyed innocence that artist Norman Rockwell made famous in his paintings. It's Americana at its best; it portrays the simple thrill all sports fans—especially young ones—feel when they meet a hero.

When it came to sports heroes, Mantle was the ultimate. And his perform-ance in 1962 didn't do anything to change that. No, his team wasn't quite as dominant as in 1961. In fact, the '62 Yankees won 13 fewer games and hit 41 fewer homers than the '61 edition. And Mantle and Maris were hard-pressed to keep up their torrid power pace: "The Mick" ended up 24 homers shy of his

This timeless portrait wasn't used by Sport *until three years after Sweet created it.*

1961 total, while Roger hit 28 fewer roundtrippers.

Still, Mantle's 30 home runs (in just 123 games) and Maris' 33 ranked them both among the top seven AL home run hitters of 1962. Mantle also hit .321, drove in 89 runs, and scored 96 in earning his third MVP award. (Actually, Mantle nearly won an unprecedented *five* MVPs: He lost by exactly one first-place vote in both 1960 and 1961.)

Most important, Mantle helped propel the 1962 Yankees—winners of 96 games—back into the World Series. Once there, New York met the San Francisco Giants in one of the most thrilling Fall Classics ever, a seven-game series capped by a 1-0 Yankee victory. The Series hero wasn't Mantle (.120, no home runs) or Maris (.174, one homer). Instead, it was the man who had been victimized in New York's epic loss in the 1960 Series: Ralph Terry.

• • •

By the early 1960s, Mantle was a hero to millions of American boys, a fact not lost on Sweet.

Every kid dreams of getting carried off the field on his teammates' shoulders after winning a World Series. Ralph Terry, who won 23 games in 1962, experienced that thrill on October 16 after throwing a four-hit shutout against the Giants, a team that boasted such power hitters as Willie Mays, Willie McCovey, and Felipe Alou.

It was a game that almost got away. In the ninth inning, with two outs, the Giants put runners on second and third with McCovey at the plate. Manager Houk decided to stick with Terry. The imposing McCovey, a 6-foot-4 future Hall

of Famer, drilled a long line drive down the right field line, but it curved foul. Then he ripped another line drive—this one right at second baseman Bobby Richardson. The Yankees won, and Terry's teammates hoisted him up and carried him off the field.

The following spring, Ozzie Sweet traveled to Ft. Lauderdale to re-create the moment. He arranged for a trio of young Yankees (from left in photo on p. 144: pitchers Roland Sheldon, Hal Stowe, and Jim Bronstad) to pose with a victorious Terry. "The fellas who are carrying him, none of them are professional actors," Sweet says. "But look how believable these guys are making it seem. Boy, are they proud of this guy! This is a good example of simulated action."

Sweet points out that cooperation from each of the players in the photo was paramount. "If one guy's not working, it spoils the whole thing. But they got it.

Sweet used a trio of non-descript young Yankees to re-create the greatest moment of Ralph Terry's career.

Look at those faces, all of 'em.

"What I'd do for this type of shoot, you know, is I'd shout at them. I'd be yelling, 'Let it go! Open your mouth! Yeah! Wow!' and they'd get right into it."

Sweet also shot an intimate portrait of Terry (p. 145) as well as a pitching series. The frame on p. 146 "really accentuates how long" the 6-foot-3 Terry's legs are, Sweet notes.

In 1963, Terry posted another credible season for New York, going 17-15 with a 3.19 ERA and 18 complete games. But he got roughed up in 1964 (7-11, 4.54 ERA) and was peddled after that season to Cleveland, where he rebounded to finish at 11-6. In 1966, he played for the Athletics and the Mets, and he retired from baseball early in the 1967 season with 107 wins in his 12 years.

• • •

For Mickey Mantle, 1963 brought more injuries. The problems started in early June at Baltimore's Memorial Stadium. On a long drive by Brooks Robinson, Mantle raced to the chainlink fence in the outfield and tried to scale it. His spikes got caught in the fence, and when he came down, his foot didn't. The painful result: a broken left foot and damaged cartilage and ligaments in his left knee.

Terry looked especially imposing when photographed from a low angle.

Despite losing Mantle for much of the season, New York coasted to another AL pennant in 1963, going 104-57 to finish 10½ games ahead of the second-place Chicago White

Fresh off the mound, Ford's face glistened with real sweat for this series of photos.

Sox. Helping to pick up the slack for "The Mick" in '63 was Elston Howard. The catcher broke the color line on the Yankees in 1955, spent a couple of seasons as a platoon player, and in 1960 became the everyday catcher when Yogi Berra moved to the outfield. In 1963, Howard jelled, hitting .287 with 28 home runs and 85 RBI while earning the AL's MVP award.

The 1963 Yankees also got power from second-year men Joe Pepitone (27 home runs) and Tom Tresh (25 homers). And Roger Maris—while he didn't come close to his 1961 season—still hit 23 home runs in only 312 at-bats.

The pitching staff, of course, was again paced by Whitey Ford. Ford finished 24-7 with a 2.74 ERA in 1963. He was joined by another 20-game winner, second-year man Jim Bouton (21-7), plus Ralph Terry (17-15) and rookie Al Downing (13-5, 2.56 ERA). The Yankees also had a steady spot starter in Stan Williams, a 6-foot-5 right-hander acquired from the Dodgers in November 1962 for another of Mantle's close friends, "Moose" Skowron. Williams won

Mantle In '63

Regular Season

Hitting

AVG	G	AB	R	H	RBI	2B	3B	HR	BB	SO	SB	OBA	SLG
.314	65	172	40	54	35	8	0	15	40	32	2	.443	.622

Fielding

POS-G	PO	A	E	DP	AVG
OF-52	99	2	1	0	.990

World Series

Hitting

AVG	G	AB	R	H	RBI	2B	3B	HR	BB	SO	SB	SLG
.133	4	15	1	2	1	0	0	1	1	5	0	.333

Noteworthy

- On May 22, Mantle hits tape-measure home run off Kansas City Athletics pitcher Bill Fischer. The ball was still rising as it hit façade in right field at Yankee Stadium—the closest any blast has ever come to completely leaving Yankee Stadium.
- Mantle crashes into chainlink fence in Baltimore on June 5 and misses most of season with a broken foot and ligament damage to left knee. He misses All-Star game in July, and doctors tell him he won't return in '63.
- August 4—With Yankees trailing 10-9 to Baltimore in second game of doubleheader, Mantle hobbles to the plate as a pinch-hitter in the 7th inning. In his first at-bat since the June injury, he lines 0-1 pitch from George Brunet into the left-field stands for a home run.

The Yankees In 1963

Won-Lost	Finish	Manager	World Series
104-57	1st place	Ralph Houk	Lost to Los Angeles Dodgers, 4 games to 0.

nine games for the '63 Yanks.

The big draw on this staff, though, was Ford—hence his participation in another session of Ozzie Sweet portraits for *Sport*. For the images reproduced on pp. 148 and 151, Sweet used his—and *Sport*'s —favorite backdrops: "Red and yellow again—just plain, no-seam, colorful backgrounds," Ozzie says. "That way, you get hit with the player first, but you also have that extra space for the [magazine's] cover lines."

Of the yellow-backed shot on p. 148, Sweet recalls: "I photographed Whitey after he'd been working out. See the sweat dripping off his chin? That's honest sweat. I've oiled up players for this type of shot, but that's real sweat here."

• • •

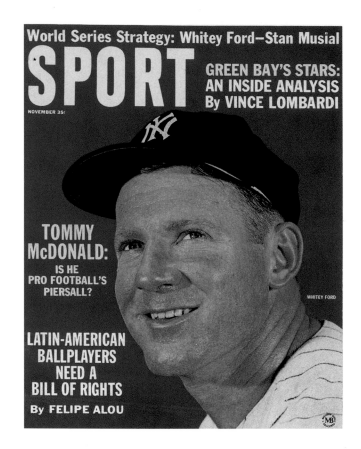

If there were a positive side to Mickey Mantle's injury-shortened 1963 season, it was the realization that baseball fans were finally in his corner. "Something was going on that season, maybe sympathy for the injuries, or just a reaction to my having been around for 13 seasons," he wrote in *All My Octobers*. "I was getting applauded and cheered in rival ballparks. In Yankee Stadium, I was getting ovations."

On August 4, Mantle returned from his June injury to pinch-hit in Game 2

Sweet had magazine covers in mind as he composed many of his most memorable portraits.

150

of a doubleheader at home against Baltimore. The Orioles won Game 1 and were leading, 10-9, in the seventh inning of the second game when Houk called on Mantle to face lefty George Brunet. On the second pitch, Mickey jumped on a fastball and sent it like a bullet over the left-field fence. The 38,000 fans in Yankee Stadium went wild: "It actually gave me chills," Mantle told reporters after the game. "I was shaking. I could feel the bumps rising on my arms."

Mantle finished the year with 15 homers in 172 at-bats, a pace that would have put him in the upper 40s over a full season.

While Mantle's 1963 regular season had a few highlights mixed with the frustrations of waiting out injuries, the World Series that year was thoroughly forgettable, at least for New York. The Yankees finally had Mantle back in the lineup for the Series, but they were pitted against Walter Alston's pitching-heavy Los Angeles Dodgers. It didn't take long for onlookers to see that New York was overmatched:

- Sandy Koufax pitched a six-hitter to win Game 1 by a 5-2 score;
- Johnny Podres and Ron Perranoski combined for a seven-hitter to win Game 2, 4-1;
- Don Drysdale pitched a three-hit shutout to win game 3, 1-0; and
- Koufax pitched another six-hitter to win Game 4, 2-1.

The Yankees' only run in the final game was a Mantle homer off Koufax, but it was no consolation for No. 7. He had only one other hit in the Series and finished with a paltry .133 average. As a team, the Yankees weren't much better, batting .171 and striking out 37 times in the four games. Roger Maris, only two years removed from his record season, had no hits in five at-bats.

Suddenly, the Yankees didn't seem so intimidating.

After a decade of playing in pain, Mantle began feeling the wear and tear.

• • •

Because he began his career in the considerable shadow of Joe DiMaggio, Mickey Mantle knew the pressure of constant comparisons to a Yankee legend. By the early 1960s, the tables were turned and Mantle was the legend by whom prospects were measured. If you were a young and athletic shortstop-turned-outfielder who could switch-hit and who possessed power as well as some speed, you'd draw the inevitable comparisons to No. 7.

Such was the case for Tom Tresh, the son of former Chicago White Sox and Cleveland Indians catcher Mike Tresh.

After a cup of coffee with the Yankees in 1961, Tresh made the team in 1962, playing 111 games at shortstop and 43 in the outfield. His numbers were impressive: 622 at-bats, 178 hits, 20 home runs, 94 runs, 93 RBI, and a .286 average. He went on to lead the Yankees in hitting (.321) in their dramatic seven-game World Series win over the Giants.

In the spring of 1963, *Sport* sent Ozzie Sweet to Ft. Lauderdale to get some pictures of this phenom. Sweet tried a different angle with Tresh, capturing him in a series of simulated-action shots from behind the plate—a catcher's-eye view. In one shot (opposite), Sweet had Tresh looking back in anger, as if he were upset with a bad call by an umpire ("You call that a strike?!"). In another (p. 156), he had him arguing the call. In still another (p. 157), he caught Tresh in a home-run-swing follow-through.

Sweet is especially proud of his "looking back" shot.

More simulated action: Tom Tresh "argues" a called strike.

"To me, everything about this—his expression, the strength in his arm, his grip on the bat, the angle of his body, the composition —is pleasing. And it's not possible unless you have somebody who can turn it on like that. And Tom did it. Of course, if you're the director, you have to find a way to get it out of the subject. Not to say that I'm a good director, but you have to have a certain

amount of skill in that area to get these guys to perform."

Tresh also was convincing as a disgruntled batter...

While Tresh never made it onto the cover of *Sport*, he did go on to post a few more productive seasons with the Yankees. In 1963, he had 25 home runs, 91 runs, 71 RBI, and a .269 average. In 1964, he posted 16 homers, 75 runs, 73 RBI, and a .246 average, plus 13 steals. And in 1965, his numbers were 26/94/74/.279. The following season, Tresh hit a career-high 27 HRs, but his batting average started slipping—down to .233 in 1966, to .219 in 1967, and finally to an anemic .195 in 507 at-bats in 1968, Mantle's final season.

The Yankees gave up on Tresh in 1969, shipping him to Detroit for out-

...and a home run hitter.

fielder Ron Woods. Tresh finished the season as a Tiger, hitting .211, before hangin' 'em up at age 32. He finished with 153 career home runs (and four more in three World Series) and a .245 average.

So Tresh wasn't "the next Mantle" after all. But he remains an intriguing character whose face is preserved in Sweet's unique catalog.

Where have you gone, Tom Tresh?

• • •

In 1964, Ozzie Sweet set out to produce another set of Mickey Mantle portraits. His session that year resulted in a warm, honest series that gives us yet another intimate look into Mantle's soul, this time as he entered the twilight of his career.

The image of Mantle holding his glove (opposite) gives him a certain innocence and a touch of anticipation. (This shot appeared as the cover of *Legends of the Field*, Sweet's 1993 book of sports photography.) The image at left is a variation; note how Mantle tilted his head ever so slightly on this one, giving it a more relaxed feel.

This 1964 session produced several warm shots of Mantle.

For the offering on p. 160, Sweet creeps in closer for a straightforward portrait. Mantle adds a slight grin on this one and holds it for an even tighter shot on p. 161. If he looks confident and self-assured in these two pictures, he takes on a shy, almost sheepish look in the shot on p. 163, a still-tighter close-up. You can almost hear him saying in his recognizable drawl, "Geez, why do people want to look at my face?"

In reference to the third image in this series (p. 160), Sweet explains: "It's just a head shot—there's not much [to it]. When you do something like this, you don't want any equipment showing—a bat, or hands around the face, or anything else. I think it's good to stay in tight, don't you?"

We do. That's why the tightest shot here (p. 163) is the most intriguing. "It's the same thing here," Sweet says. "Everything's needle-sharp, but the ears fall off. How many times do you get this close of a look at a famous face?"

Around the time these photographs were taken, Mantle launched into what would be his last spectacular season. In 1964, he played 143 games—his most since 1961. And he hit the cover off the ball, blasting 35 home runs and driving in 111 runs. He also hit .303—his 10th (and final) season with a .300 average.

With Joe Pepitone hitting 28 homers and driving in 100 runs, and with Roger Maris adding 26 home runs and 71 RBI, the Yankees proved they still had some life in their bats. And the pitching was good enough to keep the Yanks just ahead of the second-place Chicago White Sox. In fact, New York, now managed by Yogi Berra (Houk had moved upstairs as general manager) finished the season a game ahead of the White Sox.

In the World Series, the Yankees encountered a well-balanced St. Louis

Sweet's tack-sharp close-ups showed every detail in the aging slugger's face.

Cardinals squad that boasted a balanced mix of power (Bill White and Ken Boyer), speed (Lou Brock and Curt Flood), and pitching (Bob Gibson, Ray Sadecki, and Curt Simmons).

Sadecki and the Cardinals won Game 1, but the Yankees came back to take Game 2 behind rookie star Mel Stottlemyre, who had posted a 2.03 ERA and 9-3 record after being called up in August. That set up a pivotal Game 3 in New York—and the chance for Mantle to supply more Fall Classic heroics. With the score tied at 1-1 in the bottom of the 9th, "The Mick" strolled to the plate and ripped relief pitcher Barney Schultze's first offering into the right-field seats.

The euphoria didn't last long. St. Louis used a grand slam by Boyer to win Game 4 and a three-run, 10th-inning homer by Tim McCarver to win Game 5.

New York evened things up in the sixth game. The highlights included back-to-back home runs by Maris and Mantle in the 6th inning and a grand slam by Pepitone in the 8th.

So the championship came down to Game 7 in St. Louis. The Cardinals sent Gibson to the mound and the Yankees countered with Stottlemyre. New York out-homered the Cards, three to two, but Gibson made his pitches count and finished with a complete-game nine-hitter. St. Louis won the game 7-5 and the Series 4-3.

One of the home runs in Game 7 came off the bat of Mantle. It was his 18th career World Series homer—a record. In fact, Mantle was spectacular throughout the Series, batting .333, scoring eight runs, and driving in eight. It would be his final Fall Classic.

Mantle left behind a host of World Series records. Besides the home run mark (once owned by Babe Ruth, who had 15), Mickey established career highs for total bases (123), RBI (40), walks (43), and—on the negative side—strikeouts (54).

• • •

Mantle In '64

Regular Season

Hitting

AVG	G	AB	R	H	RBI	2B	3B	HR	BB	SO	SB	OBA	SLG
.303	143	465	92	141	111	25	2	35	99	102	6	.426	.591

Fielding

POS-G	PO	A	E	DP	AVG
OF-132	217	3	5	1	.978

World Series

Hitting

AVG	G	AB	R	H	RBI	2B	3B	HR	BB	SO	SB	SLG
.333	7	24	8	8	8	2	0	3	6	8	0	.792

Noteworthy

• *On August 12, Mantle hits homers from both sides of the plate in the same game for 10th and final time of his career.*
• *Mantle finishes season with league's highest on-base percentage, and also posts his last 100-RBI season.*
• *On October 10, the first of three 1964 World Series home runs put him ahead of Babe Ruth as the all-time leader.*
• *On October 15, Mantle hits the last of 18 career World Series home runs in Game 7 off St. Louis ace Bob Gibson.*

The Yankees In 1964

Won-Lost	Finish	Manager	World Series
99-63	1st place	Yogi Berra	Lost to St. Louis Cardinals, 4 games to 3.

Chapter 4

Twilight
of a Hero

1965–1968

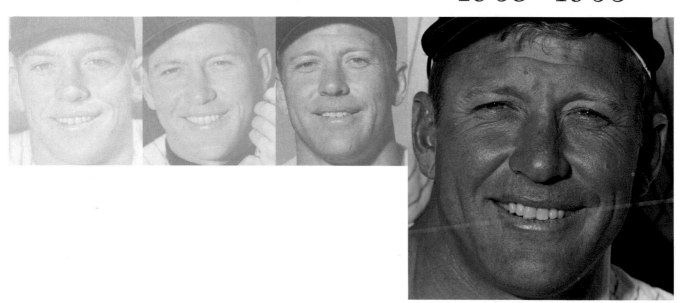

O f all the Mickey Mantle photographs Ozzie Sweet created between 1952 and 1968, there's one that meant more to the Yankee center fielder than any other.

"Mickey's favorite photo—and one of mine—was the one where his back is facing you, and you can see his No. 7, and he's leaning on his bat," Sweet says. "All baseball players lean on their bats, of course, but nobody leaned quite like Mickey did. Not only could he play better than anyone, he even leaned on his bat better than anyone!"

In assessing the photo, Sweet points out: "See the nice rhythm? You can work out a 'Z' in the way he's leaning. You see the 7 real well, and you sure know it's Mickey Mantle.

"It was a deliberate shot," Sweet says of the natural-looking photo. "I knew how Mickey stood when he leaned on his bat—how he turned like that. So, I thought, if I shoot from the back to show his No. 7, I could still have him turn his head a little bit more and show his profile. I wanted to show the number, because his 7 had become a pretty famous number by that time."

Sweet received immediate feedback on the picture from Mantle himself. "The first time I went down to spring training after the 'leaning' shot appeared," Sweet recalls, "Mickey saw me and mentioned that he really liked it, that it was his favorite. 'We did a good job on that one, Ozzie!' he said. He always acted like we were a team."

During the session, Sweet also photographed Mantle in a similar pose from the front (p. 168). That shot boasts the same majestic feel as Mantle's favorite— thanks in part to Sweet's low angle. At the same time, it offers a better look at Mickey's face.

Still another classic from that same fruitful session captures "The Mick" in

By 1965, Mickey Mantle and No. 7 were synonymous.

Even in a relaxed pose, the focused Mantle shows a strong sense of purpose.

a kneeling position (above). Note the strong profile, the subtlety of the omnipresent bat tucked under his leg, and the prominence of Mantle's muscular neck. This photo also features a rarity for a Sweet picture—a wooden fence in the background. As discussed earlier, Ozzie preferred to keep his backgrounds free of anything but the sky or a colorful backdrop.

• • •

The 1964 Yankees, under Yogi Berra, came within one game of a world championship. Yet within days of the team's Game 7 loss to St. Louis, New York's management fired Berra (not a popular move with the veteran players) and hired the Cardinals' manager, Johnny Keane (an even less popular move). Keane brought with him a no-nonsense, drill-sergeant approach that didn't work with the Yankees—and especially not with Mickey Mantle. Later, Mantle revealed that the situation got so bad he thought of retiring after the 1965 season, and might have if he'd been financially set.

Under Keane, the Yankees nose-dived to sixth place. Mantle—who moved from center to left field—had his worst hitting season yet, batting .255. He played in only 122 games, but did manage to hit 19 homers. By now, leg injuries were affecting his play, and the team's fortunes were affecting his enjoyment of baseball. That season, he told *Sport* magazine (August 1965 issue): "I feel good when I hit, and I still get a great kick out of hitting a home run, maybe a bigger kick than ever. The game is enjoyable when I'm going good, but I'm not going good. I hate to embarrass myself."

Despite Mantle's mood, his teammates looked up to him more than ever. "He's our inspiration," second baseman Bobby Richardson told *Sport*. "He doesn't realize it. I just wish he were healthy." Elston Howard told reporters, "Mickey is the spirit of this team. He makes us want to win. He fights hard all the time, and with all those injuries he ought to be in the hospital."

The Yankees organization showed its appreciation for No. 7 by hosting a Mickey Mantle Day at the Stadium. It was September 18, 1965, and 50,000 fans showed up to pay tribute. In his address, Mantle thanked the fans and the Yankees, and told the crowd he wished he could play 15 more years. And he thought of his father, who died so young in 1952. "If you fans won't mind," he

Mantle cradled his bat as if it were his best friend.

170

said, "it would make me happy if all your gifts, all the gifts you have given me, all your donations, were turned over to the Hodgkin's Disease Foundation."

During the 1965 season, Ozzie Sweet produced several new Mantle images—among them a series of portraits set against a yellow background. They're similar to Sweet's 1962 shots, which appear on pp. 141–143. In this series, though, Mantle wears the Yankees' away jersey (he wore the team's home pinstripes in the 1962 session), and he offers up a smile that belies the state of his team that season.

The focus in these 1965 shots is remarkably sharp, as you can tell by the detail in Mantle's face, hands, and cap. These particular photographs, like many of Sweet's efforts, give Mantle the look of a hero, an image he would maintain even during his lesser seasons.

One anecdote from the 1965 season, as reported in *Sport*, illustrated Mantle's lofty status in baseball circles. Al Kaline, the great Tiger right fielder who would eventually earn his own place in the Hall of Fame, was signing autographs in a Detroit department store when a young fan taunted him with the remark, "You're not half as good as Mickey Mantle." Kaline's response: "Son, *nobody* is half as good as Mickey Mantle."

• • •

Mantle's smile seemed more genuine late in his career, when he finally heard long-overdue cheers in every city.

One indication of how popular Mickey Mantle had become by the mid-1960s was a growing interest in his memorabilia. For legions of young fans who bought the latest Topps baseball cards, "The Mick" was the player to get. Pulling Mantle out of a pack was an indescribable thrill—and not because anyone knew how valuable his cards would become. Owning a Mantle card meant you had a keepsake of baseball's most visible, heroic player.

Likewise, Mantle's signature was the autograph to get. Throughout his career, he faced non-stop requests from fans to write down his name on baseballs, photos, programs, yearbooks, napkins, and countless other items. And demand for Mantle's "sig" didn't end when he retired. Fans—as they had when Mantle was a player—lined up at card shows, restaurants, hotel lobbies, and other public places hoping to get an autograph of their hero.

Mantle never understood the appeal of an autograph, but he learned to joke about it, as evidenced by this story he made up for the press (as related in *Mickey Mantle/The American Dream Comes to Life*): "I told them that I'd dreamed...I'd died and gone to heaven. I finally got in to see God and God said, 'Well, Mick, I'm sorry, but we can't keep you up here because of the way you acted on earth.' Then he said, 'Would you do me a favor?' I said, 'What's that, God?' He said, 'Before you go, would you sign those two dozen baseballs there for me?'"

Ozzie Sweet vividly remembers the hordes of fans who followed Mantle during his playing days. "I used to wander around and take [candid shots] at spring training," he says. "With Mickey, wherever he went, people wanted his autograph, especially in his later years. And he usually handled it well."

Sweet captured a typical Mantle frenzy in the mid-1960s—a black-and-white image that appears on the facing page. "I was grabbing some shots and the fans were crowding in on him," Sweet says. "And those are real fans, too; I didn't have anything to do with setting this one up."

Kids weren't the only ones interested in Mantle—even adults wanted a piece of "The Mick."

• • •

175

As he reviewed his Mickey Mantle catalog for this book, Ozzie Sweet pointed out a peculiarity in the Yankee star's attire. "Maybe you know about how Mickey used the same helmet for a long time," he says, referring to the photo at right. "I think it's interesting the way the helmet's beat up, with all of those marks and the scratches and the worn-out Yankee emblem."

The photo is a disarmingly tight close-up of Mantle in which the well-weathered helmet becomes a predominant element. "It's the only close-up I ever did of him with his helmet on," Sweet says. "And the way it sits right down on his head—there's something kind of appealing about it. He looks a little different with that on than he does with a cap on."

Sweet remembers using a long, 12-inch lens to create this Mantle portrait. It allowed him to capture every detail: "Look at his teeth. Are they sharp? Look at his lips. Look at his eyes. Every wrinkle. Have you ever seen anything so damn sharp? Of course, your range of focus when you use a long lens like that, especially in close, is barely an inch-and-a-half or two inches. I'll show you how I mean that. Look at the focus on his ear compared to his eye—his ear is out of focus. But you don't mind that, because everything important here is sharply focused."

Sweet captured Mantle in a beat-up batting helmet he wore for years.

• • •

Mantle In '65

Regular Season

Hitting

AVG	G	AB	R	H	RBI	2B	3B	HR	BB	SO	SB	OBA	SLG
.255	122	361	44	92	46	12	1	19	73	76	4	.380	.452

Fielding

POS-G	PO	A	E	DP	AVG
OF-108	165	3	6	0	.966

Noteworthy

• On April 9, Mantle hits the first home run in Astrodome history in an exhibition game against the Houston Colt .45s.
• In June, Mantle suffers a torn hamstring that causes him to miss 40 games.
• After the season, Mantle injures his shoulder playng touch football and contemplates retirement.

The Yankees In 1965

Won-Lost	Finish	Manager	World Series
77-85	6th place	Johnny Keane	Did not play.

The 1966 Yankees plunged to depths the franchise hadn't seen in decades. The season began with just four wins in the first 20 games and the firing of manager Johnny Keane. (Eight months later, Keane passed away due to heart failure.)

To replace Keane, Ralph Houk stepped down from his GM role to resume on-field responsibilities. While Houk's record was a little better (66-73) than Keane's, it wasn't enough to keep New York out of the American League cellar. By now, the Yankees had numerous holes. This clearly was a team faced with declining talent.

Whitey Ford, now 37, battled a sore arm and appeared in just 22 games in 1966. Despite a 2.47 ERA, his record was 2-5. Roger Maris' production fell to 13 home runs and a .233 average, and Elston Howard's to six homers and a .256 average. Bobby Richardson scored only 71 runs, his lowest total since 1960, and batted a disappointing .251. Longtime shortstop Tony Kubek had retired after the 1965 season and was replaced by inconsistent rookie Horace Clarke, who hit .266 and scored only 37 runs in 312 at-bats. Clete Boyer, the Yanks' third baseman since 1959, showed why he was known more for his smooth fielding than his hitting (.240 with 14 home runs in 1966). Joe Pepitone (31 homers) and Tom

Mantle In '66

Regular Season

Hitting

AVG	G	AB	R	H	RBI	2B	3B	HR	BB	SO	SB	OBA	SLG
.288	108	333	40	96	56	12	1	23	57	76	1	.392	.538

Fielding

POS-G	PO	A	E	DP	AVG
OF-97	172	2	0	0	1.000

Noteworthy

- *Between June 28 and July 8, Mantle connects for nine home runs in 11 days.*
- *For only the third time since his rookie season in 1951, Mantle is not selected to AL All-Star team.*
- *Mantle plays 97 errorless games in the outfield.*

The Yankees In 1966

Won-Lost	Finish	Manager	World Series
70-89	(10th place)	Johnny Keane/Ralph Houk	Did not play.

*The classic Mantle
follow-through.*

Tresh (27 homers) supplied power but hit only .255 and .233, respectively.

As for Mantle, he continued battling the aches and pains caused by a history of leg injuries—not to mention the shoulder injury he suffered playing touch football with his brothers during the off-season. Even so, he upped his batting average by 33 points over the previous season. He also increased his home run

total back into the 20s—and he did it only 108 games. Mantle's 23 roundtrip-

pers gave him 496 in his career, moving him past Lou Gehrig (493) and into sec-

ond place behind Babe Ruth on the all-time Yankee list.

Meanwhile, Ozzie Sweet created more simulated action Mantle shots. Among

them was the series presented on pp. 179–182. This group of photographs gives us

No matter what type of pose Mantle struck, there's no mistaking his intensity.

a look at Mantle from just in front of home plate.

"You might call it a 'worm's-eye' view," Sweet says, smiling. "I got him preparing to hit, in mid-swing, and later in his swing."

In the opening shot (p. 179), Sweet depicts Mantle as if he were standing on deck, preparing to loosen up with a handful of lumber. In two other photos from this series, Mantle offers an update of his follow-through, a pose he had struck for Sweet in earlier years. The follow-through on p. 180 is a pleasing enough simulation, albeit slightly strained compared to the image on p. 181. The latter variation—again, taken practically from Mantle's shoetop—looks more natural. The turn of his body emphasizes Mantle's powerful thighs, upper torso, and neck. Plus, the "acting" Sweet speaks of is obvious here; Mickey's eyes are following the ball into the upper deck.

The photo on p. 182 features a pose rarely associated with Mantle. Sweet meant to catch Mantle's position just after he'd lined a base hit up the middle, like he's about to drop the bat and take off to first. But this shot also looks as if it could be a bunt attempt. Either way, the power and strength we see in so many other Mantle/Sweet collaborations is missing here.

On the plus side, the angle here is interesting because Mantle leans directly over the camera. And he gives us one of those great facial expressions—a look of game intensity.

● ● ●

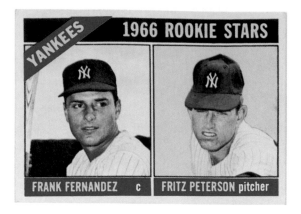

With Mickey Mantle in the twilight of his career, the Yankees began rebuilding. The result: A slew of prospects would get their shots at making a mark on the late-1960s Yankees. Some would stick; some would struggle; some would be shipped off to other teams; still others would fade into baseball oblivion.

Ozzie Sweet took the opportunity to photograph a group of Yankee hopefuls with the team's top dog, a hero to most of them. Bobby Murcer, in particular, idolized Mickey, and quickly inherited the label "The Next Mantle." The media loved to point out similarities between the two. Both hailed from Oklahoma, both were signed by scout Tom Greenwade, and both started out as shortstops before their errant fielding and throwing forced a move to the outfield.

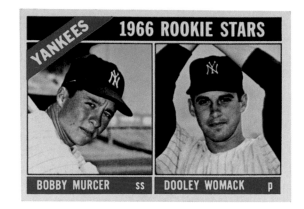

Late in the 1966 season, Sweet set up an appointment to photograph Murcer and three other rookies in a group portrait with Mantle. The fruits of that session (pp. 185, 187, and 189) include some of the finest pieces in Sweet's catalog.

In the first frame, Mantle poses in the center of the four bright-eyed, fresh-faced Yankee rookies. Clockwise from upper right are Murcer (20 years old at the time), Frank Fernandez (23), Fritz Peterson (24), and Dooley Womack (27). Technically, the picture is exquisite: a top-lit, crisp shot with vibrant, true colors.

Four New York youngsters look thrilled to pose with "The Magnificent Yankee."

184

Aesthetically, it boasts a certain charm, mainly because the boys seem to exude a sense of honest admiration for their 34-year-old mentor while Mantle looks relaxed and confident.

"They're surrounding him: He's the center of interest among all these other players," Sweet says. "And look at all these nice faces. They all have such believable, nice smiles, and they all have beautiful teeth, too. It was just very fortunate. Being a photographer, you're more apt to notice something like that. Plus, it was later in the season, so they had all picked up some color."

On p. 187 is a variation of the group shot. In this one, Sweet makes Mantle the focal point. In fact, note how the focus on the other Yanks has faded out. Sweet went so far as to crop the sides of Peterson's and Fernandez's mugs—"as long as you don't cut off their eyes," he says.

On p. 189, Sweet crops in even tighter, filling the frame with Mantle's smiling face. He uses the rookies' uniforms to create a powerful backdrop of Yankee pinstripes. This photo is, as Sweet puts it, "beautifully rich." In fact, Ozzie still marvels over it: "Look at that. Son-of-a-gun, look at his eyes—they're sharp as a tack. And he looks the way I liked to see him—he looks like a bit of a scalawag there."

Indeed, with that almost impish grin, Mantle looks like he might have just gotten into trouble. In fact, during a 1994 interview, Mantle himself reviewed the picture, as it appeared on the September 1994 issue of *Tuff Stuff*, and pointed to his eyes and the lines on his forehead: "That's from drinkin' too much."

In 1966, Mantle approached—and eventually passed—the 500-home-run mark. Meanwhile, the four freshmen with whom he posed were just getting used to major league life. Peterson and Womack each made an immediate impact. Peterson, a lefty, had an outstanding rookie season, starting 32 games, completing 11, and posting a 12-11 record and 3.31 ERA. He allowed only 196 hits in 215

innings. Womack—whose real name was Horace Guy Womack—was a right-hander who pitched out of the bullpen in all but one of his 42 appearances in 1966. He finished with a 7-3 record and a 2.64 ERA, allowing only 52 hits in 75 innings.

The pitchers' careers would follow different paths in the ensuing years. Womack had another decent season in 1967 (5-6, 2.41 ERA in 65 appearances) and a respectable year in 1968 (3-7, 3.21 ERA, but only 53 hits allowed in 62 innings). After the '68 campaign, though, the Yankees traded him to Houston for outfielder Dick Simpson. In August of 1969, the Astros traded him to the expansion Seattle Pilots for Jim Bouton, another former Yankee. Womack still put up worthy middle-relief numbers that season: a 4-2 record with a 3.31 ERA. In 1970, he played briefly for Oakland; by 1971, his playing career was over.

Peterson, meanwhile, followed his excellent rookie season with an 8-14 record in 1967. In 1968, however, he emerged as a reliable starter and began a string of winning seasons. He was 12-11 with a 2.63 ERA in 1968; 17-16 with a 2.55 ERA in 1969; 20-11 with a 2.91 ERA in 1970; 15-13 with a 3.05 ERA in 1971; and 17-15 with a 3.24 ERA in 1972. Then, before the 1973 season, Peterson made an announcement that may or may not have led to a lack of effectiveness in the coming seasons: He and fellow Yankee lefty Mike Kekich had swapped wives and families. The Yankees dropped Kekich fairly quickly, shipping him to Cleveland that June. Peterson, after an 8-15 performance in 1973, found himself headed to Cleveland as well in April 1974. He went 9-14 that year, rebounded to 14-8 in 1975, and finished his career, at age 34, with a 1-3 record for Cleveland and Texas in 1976. Later, Peterson became a devoutly religious person active in the Baseball Chapel, an organization of Christian ballplayers.

The two hitters in Sweet's 1966 Mantle/rookies portraits, Fernandez and

Ozzie Sweet zoomed in on Mantle for this memorable portrait.

Murcer, also traveled different career paths.

Fernandez, a catcher who also played some outfield, got his first major-league action in 1967, appearing in nine games and hitting .214. In 1968, he played in 51 games and hit only .170. In 1969, he began showing some power, hitting 12 home runs in 229 at-bats. But he hit only .223, and after the season, the Yankees traded him to Oakland with Al Downing for Danny Cater and the immortal Ossie Chavarria. With the A's, Fernandez picked up where he left off: 252 at-bats, 15 homers, and a .214 average. In 1971, he bounced from Oakland to the Washington Senators to the Chicago Cubs, appearing in 39 games and hitting .128. His career ended in 1972 after three appearances with the Cubs.

Murcer tried valiantly to live up to his "next Mantle" billing, although it took him a while to get started. After brief stints with the Yankees in 1965 and '66, he got called into military service and missed the 1967 and '68 seasons. In 1969, Murcer finally got his chance, and he responded with 26 home runs and 82 RBI in 152 games. By 1970, he was the Yankees' star attraction: a center fielder who could hit and run. That year, he batted only .251 but slammed 23 homers and stole 15 bases. (He also tied a major league record in 1970 by

Mantle In '67

Regular Season

Hitting

AVG	G	AB	R	H	RBI	2B	3B	HR	BB	SO	SB	OBA	SLG
.245	144	440	63	108	55	17	0	22	107	113	1	.394	.434

Fielding

POS-G	PO	A	E	DP	AVG
1B-131	1,089	91	8	82	.993

Noteworthy

- *Mantle moves from outfield to first base to save wear and tear on ailing knees.*
- *On May 14, in the third inning of a game against Baltimore at Yankee Stadium, Mantle hits his 500th career home run.*
- *He finishes the season with 518 homers—three behind Ted Williams' career total.*

The Yankees In 1967

Won-Lost	Finish	Manager	World Series
72-90	9th place	Ralph Houk	Did not play.

homering in four consecutive at-bats.)

Murcer improved all around in 1971, batting .331 with 25 homers and 94 RBI. He continued winning over Yankee fans in 1972, achieving career highs in home runs (33), runs (102), and RBI (96). Bobby had another stellar year in 1973, batting .304 with 22 home runs and 95 RBI.

In 1974, the Bronx Bombers played their home games at Shea Stadium while Yankee Stadium underwent renovations. The move seemed to affect Murcer: He hit only 10 homers and batted .274 in 606 at-bats. That winter, the Yankees traded him to the San Francisco Giants for Bobby Bonds. It wasn't a popular move with Murcer or with most Yankee fans.

Between 1975 and 1979, Murcer played for the Giants and the Cubs, and his numbers approached their former levels: He averaged 18 homers and 84 RBI in those seasons. In June 1979, Murcer, then 33, got word he was returning to the Yankees in a trade for a minor league pitcher. While Bobby would never achieve the success he'd experienced earlier in the decade, he nonetheless provided the Yankees with some memorable moments. He finished his career in 1983 with 252 home runs and a .277 average. On August 7, 1983, the Yankees honored him with Bobby Murcer Day.

• • •

Joe Pepitone earned a reputation as a free-spirited ballplayer— the guy who introduced hair dryers into locker rooms, and who was known for enjoying the nightlife. He also had a reputation as someone who didn't take his job seriously enough. Still, he averaged 26 homers a year from 1963–66. He stayed with the Yankees until 1969, and in the four years that followed, he played for the Astros, Cubs, and Braves. He retired in 1973 at age 33, with 219 home runs and a .258 average to his credit.

Pepitone's productivity in the mid-1960s earned him a place in front of Ozzie Sweet's lens. Joe relished the opportunity. "Oh, he was a character! He'd do anything," Sweet recalls. "He seemed to love to pose. He was the kind of guy who, after you'd finish, he'd say, 'You sure you have everything you need?'"

The best Pepitone picture appears on p. 192. "Pepi" hams it up for Ozzie, pointing to the middle of the plate as if he's gesturing to the pitcher for a meatball. In fact, this 1967 photo is a case of life imitating art. The following season, on September 19, 1968, Pepitone took his place in one of Mantle's memorable anecdotes. It happened during a meaningless late-season game against Detroit. The Tigers, who would win the World Series a month later, led the Yankees, 6-0, late in the game. At the plate: Mantle, who at the time had 534 career home runs, leaving him one behind Jimmie Foxx. On the mound was Denny McLain, who would win 31 games that year. McLain decided to give Mantle a freebie—nothing too blatant, just a hittable medium fastball down the middle. He called time-out and

In 1967, Sweet captured Joe Pepitone asking for a meatball down the middle.

met with catcher Bill Freehan halfway between the mound and home plate. "Let him hit one," McLain said. "This is probably his last time at bat in Detroit."

Mantle overheard him. Just before Freehan took his spot, he asked the catcher if he heard McLain right. Freehan nodded, but Mantle didn't bite. McLain threw the first pitch in; Mantle stood there and watched a beauty go by. He turned to Freehan and asked, "Is he setting me up for something?" "No, Mick, he wants you to hit one," Freehan said. So Mantle dug in, took a mighty swing at the next pitch— and fouled it into the stands. McLain grooved another, and this time, Mantle blasted it into the upper deck and winked at McLain as he rounded the bases.

Pepitone, the next hitter, strolled to the plate and motioned for McLain to throw a gimme to him, too. McLain apparently didn't see the humor in the motion. He fired a fastball behind Pepitone's head.

• • •

In spring training of 1967, Yankee manager Ralph Houk made a decision that he hoped would prolong Mickey Mantle's career. He switched his longtime center fielder to first base, a move designed to save wear and tear on his legs.

Ozzie Sweet generally photographed Mantle with a bat, but the Yankee's defensive change prompted the rare frame on p. 194. Mantle, wearing a first baseman's mitt, cooperates to make the simulated action shot work. "The Mick" is stretching as far as his legs will allow, and his glove and eyes are focused on an imaginary low throw in the dirt. Shadows almost get in the way here, due to the bill of Mantle's cap, but the composition is classic Sweet. In fact, it looks like he may have had a magazine cover in mind. He left ample "air" over both of Mantle's shoulders as space for *Sport*'s cover lines.

Mantle switched positions in 1967, and Sweet captured him with a new tool: a first baseman's mitt.

• • •

195

Antagonistic reporters challenged Houk's move of Mantle to first base. They questioned the manager as to whether the sudden stops and starts around the bag might actually cause more stress on Mantle's legs, and they wondered whether he could adjust to a position he'd never played.

Nevertheless, Mantle, helped along by the man he replaced at first base, Joe Pepitone, made the transition in smooth fashion. He played 131 games at first base and none in the outfield. Always tough on himself, Mantle graded his play as "just adequate." But it's worth noting that in 1967, he had a .993 fielding percentage—the AL's third-highest figure (behind Norm Cash, .995, and Don Mincher, .994) among starting first basemen.

Mantle's change in '67 was one of many on the Yankees, a team that no longer included Roger Maris (traded to St. Louis), Bobby Richardson (retired), or Clete Boyer (traded to Atlanta). Early in the season, Whitey Ford hung 'em up, and later in the summer, the Yanks traded Elston Howard to Boston.

While his new position may have afforded Mantle more at-bats, it didn't guarantee he'd match his previous offensive numbers. In fact, 1967 found him struggling for uncomfortably long stretches at a time.

As long as Mantle was around, however, there would still be magical moments. Consider the afternoon of May 14, 1967. That was the day Mickey hit his 500th career home run in New York against the Orioles. The Yankees honored the occasion by creating a plaque to be mounted in the spot where the historic home run landed. The plaque reads:

"MICKEY MANTLE'S 500TH LIFETIME HOME RUN LANDED HERE. MICKEY BECAME THE SIXTH PLAYER IN BASEBALL HISTORY TO HIT 500 HOMERS. HIT OFF STU MILLER AS YANKEES BEAT BALTIMORE, 6-5."

Mantle had a shiny new batting helmet by the time this photo was taken in '67.

That home run sparked a power surge by the 35-year-old. Mantle's 500th career homer was his fourth of the season; three days later (May 17), he hit his fifth. Then he homered on three consecutive days from May 19–21. He hit three more in the week that followed. Eleven days, eight homers—just like old times.

Mantle slowed down in June (three home runs all month) but perked up in July, hitting five homers to run his total to 19. From there, he tailed off sharply, hitting only three more roundtrippers while watching his batting average sink to .245. Mantle's 22 homers on the season weren't particularly productive, either. With a weak lineup around him, he finished with only 55 RBI. As a team, the Yankees were 72-90—a ninth-place squad with only the Kansas City Athletics beneath them in the AL.

Mantle and the Yanks had fallen on hard times, but No. 7 drew rousing ovations from appreciative fans wherever he went. And he remained a prime subject for Ozzie Sweet. In '67, the pair hooked up for another set of shots that show him hitting both right-handed and left-handed. (Note the new helmet.)

In the right-handed shot (p. 196), Sweet worked around shadows in Mick's face to create a remarkably sharp photo: You can practically count the hairs on Mantle's arm.

The companion shot on p. 199 captures Mantle from the left side. If Mantle's swing had been any lower during this innovative shoot, he might have knocked Ozzie's view camera back up the middle. The picture emphasizes Mantle's beefy arms—his short-tailored sleeves help—and we can see just how well his new helmet fits. In fact, we can almost feel the texture of that pinstriped jersey.

● ● ●

This low-angle shot emphasizes Mantle's massive forearms.

After retiring, Mickey Mantle often expressed regret that because of his career, "family life was missing." For 18 years, baseball took him away from his wife Merlyn and their four sons, Mickey Jr., Danny, Billy, and David.

Late in his career, Mantle occasionally brought his family with him "on the job." The late-1960s photographs on pp. 200–202, for example, capture Mantle with Mickey Jr. during downtime in spring training. In the first image, Mantle provides his son with some fishing instructions. Ozzie Sweet didn't accompany the pair on the excursion, but he did photograph them before they left. (Note the styles of the day —the casual short-turtleneck shirt and tight-fitting slacks on Mickey and the bright red bellbottoms on Mickey Jr.) In the photo above, Sweet caught the Mantles as they prepared to take off on a boat ride.

By the late 1960s, Mantle's fishing trips included his son Mickey Jr.

In the final three images presented here, Sweet offers a look at Mickey and Mickey Jr. on the coast of Florida. The obvious shot, of course, finds the two of them striking a batting pose. "That was in Florida," Ozzie recalls, "and I shot it for *Boy's Life* magazine. Mickey brought his son down there just for the shoot."

• • •

Near the end of his life, Mantle regretted not spending more time with his family.

Late in Mickey Mantle's career, Ozzie Sweet cast a set of images that combine natural sunlight, minor flash fills, and looming shadows. Thanks to his technique and to the utter honesty of his view camera, Sweet preserved the image of Mantle's smiling face drenched in hot rays on what must have been a perfect summer day at the ballpark.

In one photo, presented on p. 205, there's a certain wistfulness to Mantle's look. In the others (pp. 206 and 207), the more prominent positioning of a couple of bats adds a rich, woody texture—and an ideal complement to Mantle's squinty smiles.

The baseball fan in all of us, of course, wishes that Mantle's waning days as a player had been happier. Instead, Mantle found himself thinking frequently of retirement in the mid- to late-1960s.

In what would be his final season, 1968, Mantle struggled at the plate, finishing the year with his lowest batting average ever—a mere .237. It was enough to drop his career mark below .300 (he ended at .298). It pained Mantle for the rest of his life to think about those two percentage points. He later would say he wished he had retired before the 1968 season.

On the other hand, "The Mick" led the Yankees in home runs (with 18) in his final year. His fourth homer of 1968 allowed him to pass one more legend on the all-time list, a man Mantle respected as much as any other ballplayer: Ted Williams. (Willie McCovey, who played until 1980, retired with the same total as Williams—521).

Mantle's 522nd home run came at Yankee Stadium on May 6, 1968, off Sam McDowell of the Indians. After the game, he told reporters, "It just gave me chills. To think that I had passed my hero, Ted Williams, in home runs was really thrilling. I couldn't get over it." At the same time, he said, "I just kept

Dramatic lighting for this photo session emphasized the twilight of Mantle's career.

thinking how proud my dad would have been of me."

Mantle hit 14 more blasts that season, including the "gift" from Denny McLain (see p. 193) for No. 535 as well as one final blast off Boston's Jim Lonborg on September 20, 1968, for No. 536. At the time, only Babe Ruth and Willie Mays had more home runs.

For Mantle, the end of his glorious 18-year career came quietly on the night of September 28, 1968. The Yankees were in Fenway Park, and Mantle, facing Lonborg again, hit a pop-up toward the left side of the infield. Shortstop Rico Petrocelli settled under the ball and squeezed it. Mantle limped back to the dugout and took a seat. Moments later, manager Houk beckoned Andy Kosco to grab his glove and head out to first base.

• • •

Even though a .237 average in '68 dropped Mantle's career average below .300, he always looked comfortable with a bat in his hands.

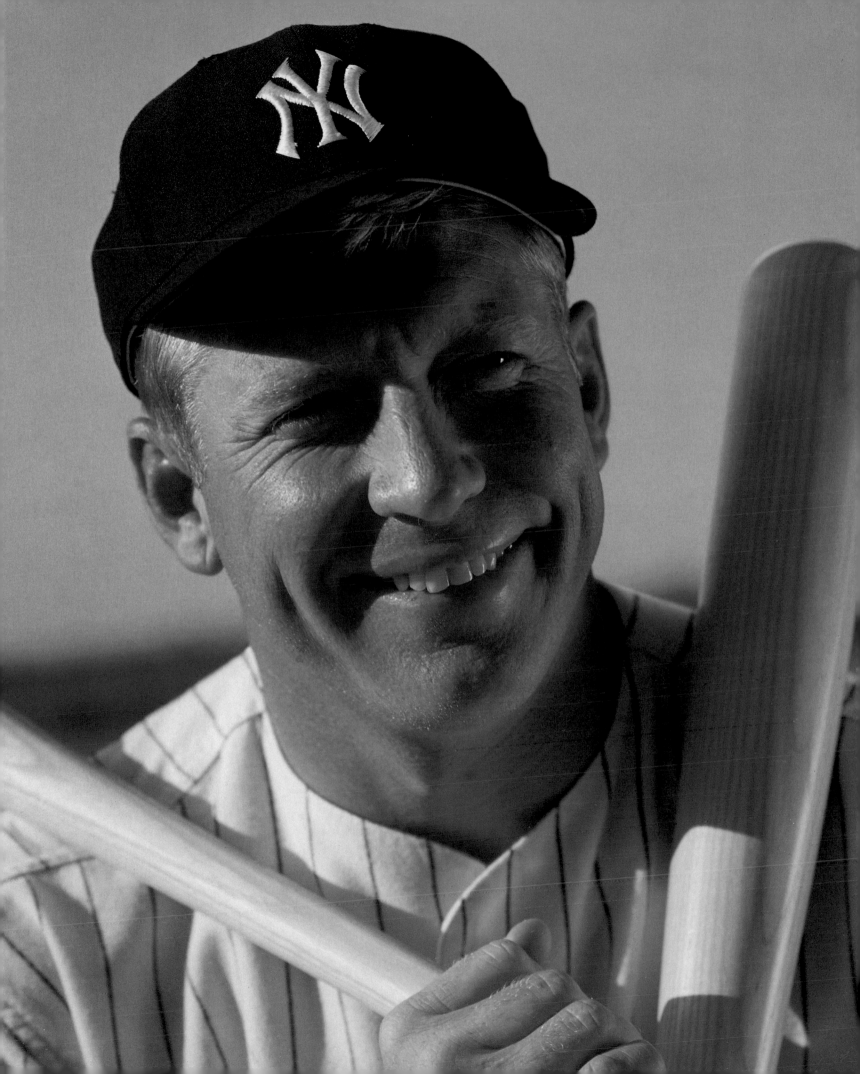

The called shot. Every baseball fan knows about that dramatic moment from the 1932 World Series, when Babe Ruth pointed to center field in Game 3 against Charlie Root and the Chicago Cubs. He followed that gesture with a home run exactly where he said he'd hit it.

There are baseball historians who insist the anecdote is a myth, that Ruth wasn't actually calling his homer when he pointed. No matter. The story has become a baseball legend passed down through the generations.

In 1968, Ozzie Sweet encouraged Mickey Mantle to mimic Ruth with his own "called shot" pose. You can tell by the smile on Mantle's face in the picture (opposite) that Mickey wasn't totally buying the concept—but he posed anyway, giving Sweet one of his more playful, irreverent frames.

Then it was back to work.

In a more serious shot from the same session (p. 210), Sweet went all out to capture Mantle in a striking, heroic pose. It's fully effective, too, with Mantle resting his weapon on his shoulder and looking out over his kingdom—the ballfield. "It gives us a nice profile, too," Sweet says. "There are no shadows, and the lighting is excellent."

Still another vintage photo taken late in Mantle's career is the swing follow-through on p. 213. The colors in this masterpiece are brilliant, the pose is convincing (note the concentration in Mantle's eyes), and the composition is flawless.

By this time, Mantle's retirement was imminent. Perhaps that's why Sweet put "The Mick" in one more heroic pose—the portrait on p. 215. This poignant image is the last picture Sweet took of Mantle as a player. It embodies all of the qualities that *Sport*'s readers had come to appreciate over the years: a solid, colorful background; a low angle; a simple pose; and tight, frame-filling composition.

Because Ozzie created this definitive portrait before Mickey retired, *Sport*

Mantle eventually achieved a hero status previously reserved for Babe Ruth. Sweet obliged him with a re-creation of Babe's called shot.

magazine had it ready for use as a cover shot the minute Mantle made his announcement. That day came on March 1, 1969 (the image appeared on the April 1969 *Sport*). Mantle had spent the off-season wondering whether he should give baseball one more go. But by March, he knew it was time to call it a career.

Sweet's "Farewell to Mickey Mantle" photograph would show up en masse at Yankee Stadium on June 8, 1969. That was the Sunday afternoon the Yankees deemed "Mickey Mantle Day." *Sport* helped make it memorable by issuing a special full-color flyer of Sweet's "Farewell" shot.

Some 70,000 people showed up to acknowledge Mantle's remarkable career. Longtime Yankee broadcaster Mel Allen (who had been dropped from his role in 1964) was back to introduce "The Commerce Comet": "That magnificent Yankee, the great number 7, Mickey Mantle!" The fans launched into a 10-minute standing ovation that died down only at the urging of Yankee president Michael Burke. An emotional Mantle told the crowd that he now understood why Lou Gehrig called himself "the luckiest man alive" on his own tribute day in 1939. The sentimental afternoon ranked as "the biggest thrill I've ever had," Mantle said later.

At the time Mantle retired, Ozzie Sweet also began thinking about new directions. After photographing athletes for 20 years, he had compiled a library of images that would define a golden era in sports. So as the new decade dawned, Sweet turned his attention to wildlife photography. He became a leader in that field, too, collaborating with writer Jack Denton Scott on a series of award-winning books. When he later turned to classic automobiles and trucks as subjects, he excelled in that pursuit as well.

As the years went by, Sweet occasionally turned his lens toward pro athletes

Mantle In '68

Regular Season

Hitting

AVG	G	AB	R	H	RBI	2B	3B	HR	BB	SO	SB	OBA	SLG
.237	144	435	57	103	54	14	1	18	106	97	6	.387	.398

Fielding

POS-G	PO	A	E	DP	AVG
1B-131	1195	76	15	91	.988

Noteworthy

- Mantle registers more walks than hits.
- On May 6, Mantle hits his 522nd home run (off Cleveland's Sam McDowell) to pass Ted Williams on the all-time list.
- Mantle's third-inning home run off Boston's Jim Lonborg on September 20 is his last. His total of 536 career roundtrippers is the highest ever for a switch-hitter. At the time, he's third on all-time homer list behind Babe Ruth and Willie Mays.
- On September 28, Mantle plays his last game. He's 36 years old—the same age as Joe DiMaggio and Lou Gehrig when they retired.

The Yankees In 1968

Won/Lost	Finish	Manager	World Series
83-79	(5th place)	Ralph Houk	Did not play.

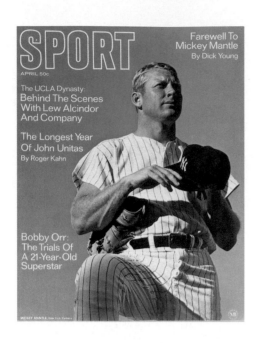

again. From time to time, he'd show up at spring training and photograph his old pals, or he'd re-create his friendly portrait style with a hot young baseball player—like Dale Murphy in 1983.

But for Ozzie, it just wasn't the same—not without that wide grin and those sparkling, smiling eyes of Mickey Mantle looking at him. And just as Mantle's retirement as a player was baseball's loss, Sweet's "retirement" from sports photography has been a loss to every fan who came to appreciate his intimate, inimitable style.

Ozzie's final portrait of Mantle was a fitting farewell shot.

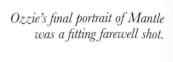

The Yankee Years

Regular season

Hitting

AVG	G	AB	R	H	RBI	2B	3B	HR	BB	SO	SB	OBA	SLG
.298	2,401	8,102	1,677	2,415	1,509	344	72	536	1,733	1,710	153	.423	.557

Fielding

POS-G					PO	A	E	DP	AVG
OF-2,019, 1B-262, SS-7, 2B-1, 3B-1					6,734	290	107	201	.985

World Series

AVG	G	AB	R	H	RBI	2B	3B	HR	BB	SO	SB	SLG
.257	65	230	42	59	40	6	2	18	43	54	3	.535

Fielding

PO	A	E	DP	AVG
126	1	3	0	.977

All-Star Games

Avg.	G	AB	R	H	RBI	2B	3B	HR
.238	15	42	5	10	4	0	0	2

Mantle Among Yankees All-Time Leaders

Category	Total	Rank	Category	Total	Rank	Category	Total	Rank
Games Played	2,401	1	Hits	2,415	3	RBI	1,509	4
At-Bats	8,102	1	Doubles	344	5	Walks	1,733	2
Runs Scored	1,677	3	Home Runs	536	2	Batting Average	.298	10

215

Old Friends

After Mickey Mantle's retirement as a player in March 1969, he withdrew from the baseball scene for a short time. In the summer of 1970, he returned to Yankee pinstripes to coach, but the gig—which involved three-inning stints in the first base coaching box—lasted just a few weeks. "The Mick" realized he was there mainly to draw people into Yankee Stadium. He later referred to his contributions as "a joke." He simply didn't have the interest in pursuing a full-time coaching career. For many years into his retirement, though, he showed up at the

Yankees' spring trainings in Florida to serve as an instructor.

By the early 1970s, Ozzie Sweet had pulled away from sports work and had begun to travel to exotic locales to photograph wildlife. Occasionally, though, Sweet would travel to Florida to visit with his old Yankees friends. He wouldn't set up and execute his old-style view-camera portraits, but he did take the time to grab some candids of the old gang, including Mickey, Yogi Berra, Whitey Ford, and Billy Martin.

The Mantle candid presented here comes from the mid-1970s. It finds

Mickey catching up with former Yankee manager Ralph Houk. (By then, Houk was managing the Detroit Tigers; he served in that capacity from 1974–78.)

Berra, after managing the Mets from 1972–75, returned to the Yankees as a coach in 1976. He would serve in that capacity until 1984, when he took over as manager and posted an 87-75 record. In 1985, after starting the season with a 6-10 mark, Yogi found himself without a job, another of George Steinbrenner's casualties.

Ford served as a Yankee pitching coach in 1964 and from 1974–75. Pictured on p. 218 in a 1974 photo, Whitey is seated alongside George "Doc" Medich. (Medich was a promising Yankee pitcher who won 14 games in 1973, 19 in 1974, and 16 in 1975. The Yankees then traded him to Pittsburgh for Willie Randolph and Dock Ellis.) Ford earned induction into baseball's Hall of Fame in 1974—the same year Mantle went in.

Martin, of course, won more notoriety in his post-playing days. He was as fiery a manager as he was a player. He began managing in 1969 with the Twins, a short-lived relationship marred by an incident in which Billy punched out 20-game-winner Dave Boswell. Martin went to the Tigers in 1971, but lasted less than three years there. He moved on to Texas, where he managed for part of 1973, all of 1974, and part of 1975. That was the year he made his dramatic return to the Yankees, taking over for Bill Virdon midway through the season. The following year, he led the Yanks to an American League championship,

In the mid-1970s, Sweet grabbed candids of Mickey Mantle (left, with Ralph Houk) and Yogi Berra at spring training.

217

and in 1977, he took them to the top—the team's first world championship in 15 years.

Around that time, Sweet photographed Martin (far right) listening intently to his former boss, Houk, who was still guiding the Tigers. This simple candid is a study in Martin's intensity and seriousness about baseball.

In 1978, Martin's running quarrel with Steinbrenner intensified. During a game against the Red Sox that season, the embattled Martin tried to attack Reggie Jackson, who he had pulled off the field in the middle of an inning for an apparent lack of effort.

Ninety-four games into the season, Martin was gone, replaced by Bob Lemon.

At left is Whitey Ford as a coach; at right is his old teammate, Billy Martin, as a manager.

Of course, Martin replaced Lemon as manager midway through the 1979 campaign, but Steinbrenner made another change after the season. Billy finally moved on to another franchise: the Oakland A's, a team he managed from 1980–83. But he wasn't finished with the Yankees yet: He would be in and out of the picture three times in the mid-1980s, managing the team in 1983, 1985, and 1988.

The latter season was his last. Sadly, he died in a car accident in December 1989.

Ford, in a mid-1970s series of honest Sweet action shots, showed he still has his form.

Index

ALLSTON

GAYLORD S